ACKNOWLEDGMENTS

To produce a book like this takes the cooperation and efforts of many dedicated people. I would like to take a moment and extend to each of them my heart-felt thanks. Without each one of you, this book would not have been possible. Special thanks to Naomi and to Steven Wybenga of Naomi's of San Francisco, David Baker, and Jean Newsome of The Antique Shop (West Chester, Pennsylvania). You were all most helpful during what has proven to be a very difficult year for this author.

I would also like to thank Molly Higgins, who diligently took down most of the caption material on the San Francisco photo shoot, and Doug Congdon-Martin and Peter Schiffer, who sent us to California in the first place. Finally, special thanks to Don and Joy Ng!

CONTENTS

INTRODUCTION

This book presents an overview of American twentieth century pottery produced during the Depression, that troubled time in American history said to have been ushered in by the Wall Street stock market crash of 1929 and swept away during the 1940s on the rising tide of World War II. The ceramics offered are a sampling of the table, kitchen, art pottery, and artwares produced by some of the many notable pottery companies of the period. The intent is to give the reader a feel for the range of wares offered to cash strapped consumers during this difficult time. It is the author's hope that once readers have become acquainted with the durable, brilliant wares produced during the Depression years, they will be inspired to explore the equally worthy pottery offerings of the other American potters and potteries from this period; potters who were excluded from this survey not for any lack of merit on their part but from a lack of space on mine.

Generally speaking, Depression era pottery was durable, affordable, vibrantly glazed ceramics of various earthenwares or special clay mixes. It was mass produced in pottery factories and decorated in a simple manner to keep costs low. In form and decoration, the vast majority of these wares had a modern and dynamic Art Deco look. However, from the kitchen and tablewares to the artwares, Depression pottery ran the spectrum from the cost effective and cheery to the costly and luxurious as you shall soon see.

WHO AND WHERE?

Very briefly, United States' consumers during the Depression years were looking for inexpensive, casual table and kitchenwares. These services were to reflect a new, informal life-style that was both trendy and necessary. Gone for the vast majority of Americans were the days of expensive formal dinner parties and the servants that carted the multiple courses to and from the table. Depression society threw simple affairs—casual dinners at which guests served them-

Bauer water carafes with lids (lids are very rare). 9" high. Black. $1600+. Orange. $800+. Delph Blue (no lid). $300. Yellow. $800+. *Courtesy of Naomi's of San Francisco.*

selves. J.A. Bauer Pottery of Los Angeles was leading the field in providing the festive, inexpensive, casual wares for the table and the kitchen, offering brightly glazed dinnerware with simply designed, durable ceramic bodies. The brightly colored glazes paid tribute to California's joint Spanish and Mexican heritage. The color, simplicity, durability, and inexpensive price of Bauer's bright wares suited the needs of Depression period consumers well.

The success of the J.A. Bauer Pottery's bright and simple wares inspired other California potteries, including Pacific and Gladding, McBean and Company, to try their hand at informal dinnerware and kitchenware. Nor was this trend to go unnoticed back East. The Homer Laughlin China Company of Newell, West Virginia, presented their take on casual dining in 1936 with the introduction of Fiesta. (Levin 1988, 170)

Fiesta would become the best known of the vibrantly colored dinnerware lines first offered during the Depression. Homer Laughlin's art director Frederick Rhead had designed his product well. The first five deep colors offered for Fiesta in 1936 were the results of careful market research. Adding to the popularity of Fiesta was the fact that this ware was priced very low, sold through F. W. Woolworth and similar outlets. This tableware was targeted straight to the working class and the working class responded enthusiastically.

Buoyed by the success of Fiesta, the Homer Laughlin China Company produced variations on this line such as Harlequin, sold exclusively through F. W. Woolworth. Fiesta colors were also added to Homer Laughlin's kitchenwares in the late 1930s as part of the company's Kitchen Kraft line. (Levin 1988, 170-171)

Turning our attentions to art pottery, back in the late 1800s ceramic painting was very popular with the ladies. In fact, the passion for ceramic painting would lead directly to the establishment of Rookwood Pottery, possibly the leading American art pottery, in Cincinnati, Ohio. Rookwood Pottery was founded in 1880 by Maria Longworth Nichols. Part of Maria Nichols's original impetus to establish this pottery stemmed from her perception that she had been snubbed by Cincinnati's Women's Pottery Club. Maria Nichols set herself up apart from the Pottery Club. In time family and friends assisted Maria Nichols in the establishment of a complete pottery factory. Rookwood Pottery was ready for operation in September 1880. (Gilchrist 1981, 116).

Vases, turned on the potter's wheel, were the most common form produced at the newly established Rookwood Pottery. Rookwood pieces were signed

Tumblers by Catalina Clay Products in various colors: Red with handle, Red, Monterey Brown ($68), Yellow ($58), Green ($68), Light Blue, Blue, Seafoam ($68), White ($48) 4" high. $45-70. *Courtesy of Naomi's of San Francisco.*

A Fiesta montage featuring the original five colors (Red, Yellow, Cobalt, Light Green, Ivory), and Turquoise (added in 1937). *Courtesy of Jean E. Newsome, The Antique Shop, West Chester, Pennsylvania.*

by their designers. In the late nineteenth century, the Rookwood patterns and glazes were greatly influenced by Japanese techniques. Rookwood wares were soon noted for striking glazes. The shimmering crystalline Tiger Eye glaze was especially admired. (Gilchrist 1981, 116)

Other potteries actively producing art pottery, and later artware, could be found throughout the United States. A number of these firms would continue production during the Depression years. Among them were Steubenville, Weller, and Roseville. W.A. Long, encouraged by the successes of Rookwood, brought Steubenville into the artware field with the introduction of a line he developed and christened Lonhuda. Samuel A. Weller, in Zanesville, Ohio, also turned to the production of wares similar to Rookwood's. Weller was creating pottery in copious amounts in 1895 and produced an eye-catching iridescent glaze combining different metallic lusters. Roseville Pottery, incorporated in Roseville, Ohio, in January of 1892, would produce its first art pottery around 1900. Roseville's most successful artware line, Pine Cone, would be first introduced during the depths of the Depression in 1935. (Gilchrist 1981, 116; Levin 1988, 68; Bassett 1999)

A MATTER OF STYLE

Art Deco was the style that was most influential between 1925 and the beginning of World War II. Geometric forms and lavish decorative techniques were the hallmarks of Art Deco. It was at the Paris Exhibition of 1925 (the *Exposition des Arts Décoratifs et Industriels Modernes*) that the public was made aware of Art Deco. Exhibitions of this sort had long been used both to show the best of modern design to the public and to give international competitors a chance to compare products and glean new trends. It became clear at the Paris exhibition that the organic Art Nouveau lines were being replaced with the geometric, streamlined forms and rich decoration of Art Deco.

The Art Deco style would reach its height of popularity and influence in 1935. In America, the Depression brought Art Deco styling to new forms. Many Americans found themselves cash-strapped and were in no mood to purchase expensive luxuries in a lavish, streamlined style. As a result, Art Deco styling was incorporated into simple, durable, mass produced wares that could be purchased for a song. (Hay 1996, 6-10)

EFFECTS OF POTTERY PRODUCTION

Before plunging into the exploration of the potteries and their wares in earnest, it is worth taking a moment to discuss some of the more common factory flaws and production by-products which may be found on pottery. While these factory flaws will lower the value of the pottery they are found on, they should not be mistakenly identified as indications that the pottery has been damaged at some time after it was produced.

When glaze has been applied to the body of any vessel, some method must be used to keep the glaze from hardening to the sagger during firing (a sagger is a protective clay box into

Roseville wares. Front: Moss candlesticks, 1930s, 2" high. $195+. Back: Velmoss vases, 1935: Left vase, 12.5" high. $450+. Right vase, 6.5" high. $175+. *Courtesy of Naomi's of San Francisco.*

which pottery is placed during kiln firing). Two common methods used to keep the glaze out of contact with the sagger are the dry foot and the stilt. The foot (for wares that have them) is that part of a ceramic object on which it rests, i.e. the base. Using the dry foot method, by carefully removing any traces of glaze from the foot prior to firing—ensuring that the foot is "dry"—the potter ensures that glaze will not come into contact with the sagger and that the pottery will not adhere to it.

If it is desirable for the bottom of a piece to be glazed, then the glazed surface may be kept out of contact with the surrounding sagger by using stilts. A stilt is a small, Y shaped bisque support, a type of "kiln furniture," with projections reaching up above and down below the Y. A pot with a glaze coated base may be placed on the stilt's projecting ends within the sagger, keeping the glazed base raised up off the bottom of the sagger. During firing, as the glaze hardens, it adheres to the stilt at those three small points. Once the firing is complete, and the kiln cooled, it is a simple matter to give the pot a quick twist to snap it free from the stilt. Left behind on the base of the pot are three glaze free tell-tale dots where the stilt supported the piece. These are called "stilt marks" and should not be mistaken for damage.

Pottery production, like life itself, does not always go smoothly. Mistakes are made and some pottery is produced with small irregularities. Depending on the standards of the potting firms involved, wares featuring small irregularities may have been overlooked entirely or they may have been sold as factory seconds. Pieces with manufacturing flaws will be valued lower in the collectibles market than their pristine brethren but such pieces once again should not be considered damaged goods.

Common factory flaws include unusual glaze color variations, visible mold seam lines, uneven bases, ill-fitting lids, and handles that do not match in proportion or placement. Glaze crazing is a common flaw. Crazing occurs when the clay body and glaze cool at different rates, creating thin cracks in the glaze. At times, pottery chipped in the bisque stage was glazed and fired anyway. On close inspection you will note in this case that the glaze completely covers the break. Along the same line, at times pots have been glazed and fired with small bits of clay adhering to an otherwise smooth surface. These clay bits should have been removed prior to glazing and firing, but were missed by the potter. Finally, "kiln kisses" occur when a pot

Bauer rare lug soup bowl, Delph Blue, 5.5". $125 (missing cover). Covered individual baker, Orange, 4.5". $85. Lug soup bowl, 6". $95. Soup plate, Maroon, 7.5". $145. Ramekin, Green, 4.5". $25. *Courtesy of Naomi's of San Francisco.*

touches either the sagger wall or another pot as it is being loaded into the sagger for firing, leaving dents or unglazed areas on the pot. (Bassett 1999)

ABOUT PRICING

The prices found in the captions are in United States dollars. Prices vary immensely based on the location of the market and the enthusiasms of the collecting community. Prices in the Midwest differ from those in the West or East, and those at specialty shows or auctions will differ from those in dealer's shops.

All of these factors make it impossible to create absolutely accurate price listings, but a guide to realistic pricing may be offered. These values are not provided to set prices in the collectibles marketplace, but rather to give the reader a realistic idea of what one might expect to pay for Depression era pottery in mint condition. Best of luck to you in your search for these colorful and exciting wares!

—Jeffrey B. Snyder

Individual Kitchen Kraft casseroles in Yellow and Light Green. 2.75" high x 4.5" in diameter. $130-140 each. *Courtesy of Jean E. Newsome, The Antique Shop, West Chester, Pennsylvania.*

See Casual Dining, page 7.

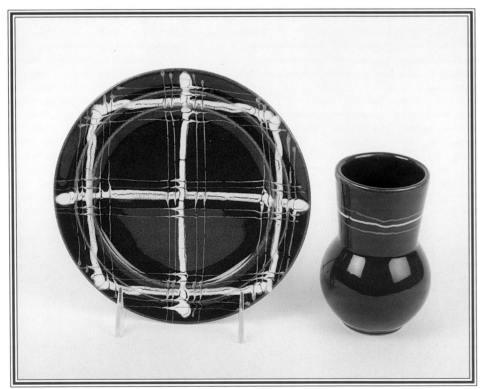

Hand-painted wares by Pacific. Plate, Cobalt, 7.5" diameter. $45. Vase, Cobalt, 5" high. $65. *Courtesy of Naomi's of San Francisco.*

Fiesta disk pitchers and tumblers. *Courtesy of Jean E. Newsome, The Antique Shop, West Chester, Pennsylvania.*

See Art Pottery & Artware History, page 7-8.

Vase by Rookwood, 1929, 7" high. $400+.
Courtesy of Naomi's of San Francisco.

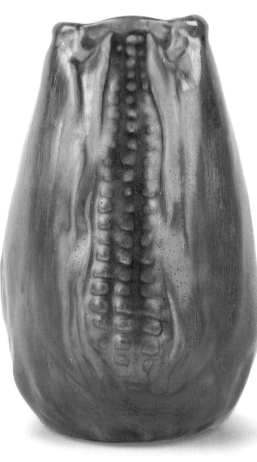

A Weller vase in the form of a corncob by
Sicard (an artist working for Weller for a
time), 1902-1907, 5" high. $825. *Courtesy
of Naomi's of San Francisco.*

Burntwood hanging basket, Weller, 1910, 3" high x 9.25" diameter.
$175. *Courtesy of Naomi's of San Francisco.*

Claywood vase and bowls by Weller, 1910. Claywood differs from Burntwood with the addition of dark brown vertical bars. Back: Vase, 5.25" high. $185. Cup with handle, 4.5" high. $125. Front: bowl, 2.5" high. $165. bowl, 3.5". $125. bowl, 2.5". $165. *Courtesy of Naomi's of San Francisco.*

Weller Blue Bottom Mat Green Glaze wares dating from c. 1910-the 1920s. Back: Vase, 5.25" high. $325. Oblong planter, 3.5" high x 9" wide. $475. Small vase, 3.5" high. $235. Front: Planter, 3.5" high x 5.75" wide. $325. Footed planter, 3.75" high, window marking. $295. *Courtesy of Naomi's of San Francisco.*

See Art Pottery & Artware History, page 7-8.

Planter with flower frog by Weller, 1910, set is 3.25" high. $265. *Courtesy of Naomi's of San Francisco.*

Orris vase, 1915, 7" high. $295. *Courtesy of Naomi's of San Francisco.*

Orris bowl, 1915, 3.25" high x 6" wide. $195. *Courtesy of Naomi's of San Francisco.*

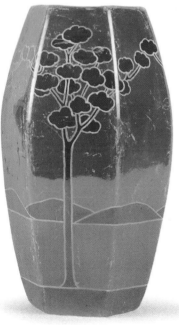

Scandia vase, 1915, 9.25" high. $495; Marengo vase (Orange), 1920-1925, 8.25" high. $395. *Courtesy of Naomi's of San Francisco.*

Velvetone pitcher by Weller, hand thrown, 1920s. $225. *Courtesy of Naomi's of San Francisco.*

Cloudburst vase, 1921, 7.5" high. $225. *Courtesy of Naomi's of San Francisco.*

See Effects of Pottery Production, page 8-10.

Note the three stilt marks. *Courtesy of Naomi's of San Francisco.*

Factory flaw, a "kiln kiss." *Courtesy of Naomi's of San Francisco.*

Pine Cone double flower holder by Roseville, 1935, 8.25" high. $395. Vase, 6" high. $395. Flower holder, 7.5" high. $175. *Courtesy of Naomi's of San Francisco.*

POTTERIES AND WARES

BAUER POTTERY

In 1909-1910, John Andrew Bauer transplanted his successful pottery firm, producing utilitarian stonewares, redware flowerpots, garden vases, mixing bowls, pie plates and other useful ceramics, from Paducah, Kentucky, to Los Angeles, California, establishing his pottery on the city's periphery in Lincoln Heights. While several of the most popular molds were also shipped from the Kentucky factory to California, the company quickly added new designs suited to California tastes to the product lines. By the 1920s, the J.A. Bauer Pottery was not only the leading Southern California producer of redware flowerpots, but was also aggressively marketing a varied array of bean pots, covered crocks, mixing bowls, nappies, and whiskey jugs, among other items. The company's most striking successes were yet to come in the 1930s. (Johnson 1996; Chipman 1999, 22.)

Around 1915, the company had hired both Louis Ipsen, a skilled designer, and Matt Carlton, a talented Arkansas potter. Together, they quickly developed an artware line for the firm. Hand thrown and molded decorative bowls and vases, most glazed in the matte green glaze fashionable at that time, made up the majority of the company's art pottery/artwares. (Johnson 1996; Chipman 1999, 22.)

J.A. Bauer died at the age of 67 in 1922, and for a time the leadership of the company was in flux. By 1929, however, Watson Bockmon, husband of J.A. Bauer's daughter Eva, was in charge. By this time, the firm had hired Victor Houser, a ceramics engineer, to create a new line of opaque colored glazes for various earthenware products, including dinnerware, flowerpots, and vases. The J.A. Bauer Company, along with others in the field, was experimenting with solid color glazes for single color, durable casual earthenware dinnerwares.

"Plain" ware, individual coffee pots by Bauer, 5.75" high. Orange. $125. Green. $125. Blue. $185. *Courtesy of Naomi's of San Francisco.*

Houser's original palate of bright glazes included Chinese Yellow, Jade Green, Orange-Red, Delph and Royal Blue, Ivory, Black, and White. However, with the advent of World War II and the shortages created by the war effort, Houser reformulated or replaced these vibrant glazes with pastel shades. (Bauer 1996, 1 & 48; Chipman 1999, 22)

Well before World War II, Louis Ipsen molded the first casual line, glazed in the bright colors Houser produced, and heralded by the company as mix-and-match sets. This plain line of "California Colored Pottery" tableware was introduced to the public in 1930. In 1932-33, Houser's and Ipsen's efforts created the "ring" ware line. Distinctive rings of closely spaced concentric circles decorated this ware's hollow forms while three concentric rings adorned the plates and platters.

With these colorful wares, the J.A. Bauer Company would be first among its peers to successfully enter the market with its offering of brightly colored, mix-and-match ceramics for the table and kitchen. It did not take consumers long to appreciate the advantages of inexpensive, casual dining.

Moving on from the success of ring ware, the company opened a second plant in 1935, when the nearby Batchelder-Wilson plant closed. With new equipment and new facilities, Bauer went on to produce additional tablewares during the Depression years, including the Monterey and La Linda lines.

Some of the fiercest competition for the casual dinnerware market came from the East. The Homer Laughlin China Company of Newell, West Virginia, introduced their brightly colored,

"Ring" ware, 10.75" plates, featuring the basic Bauer colors: Orange Red, Chinese Yellow, Cobalt, Jade Green. $110-165. *Courtesy of Naomi's of San Francisco.*

durable, and inexpensive Fiesta line in 1936. Watson Bockmon responded to the East Coast challenge by opening a new pottery factory in Atlanta, Georgia. Unfortunately, Bockmon died suddenly in 1939, just as the new plant was reaching its full production potential. The company continued after Bockmon's untimely death, with the Atlanta firm producing casseroles, teapots, and water pitchers to bolster the efforts of the Los Angeles plant. During World War II, however, the Atlanta branch turned to producing white cereal bowls and mugs for the United States Navy.

Artware would continue to be produced by the firm as well. Mold cast artwares were the responsibility of Jim Johnson and Ray Murray, featuring the single glaze colors used to such great effect on Bauer's casual dinnerwares. Matt Carlton and his nephew Fred Johnson saw to the production of wheel thrown art pottery.

During the 1950s, the J.A. Bauer Company would suffer under the combined stresses of heavy local and international competition in the pottery market. Financial difficulties ensued, leading to a crippling strike in 1961, and the company's closure in 1962. (Chipman 1999, 22-23; Bauer 1996, 1 & 48)

Monterey line by Bauer. 9" plates; Orange-Red, Royal Blue. $15. Soup bowl, Orange-Red, 7". $26.
Courtesy of Naomi's of San Francisco.

Typical Bauer Marks

Bauer Pottery USA mark. *Courtesy of Naomi's of San Francisco.*

Bauer Pottery Atlanta USA script mark. *Courtesy of Naomi's of San Francisco.*

Bauer Pottery Co. Los Angeles Cal. mark. *Courtesy of Naomi's of San Francisco.*

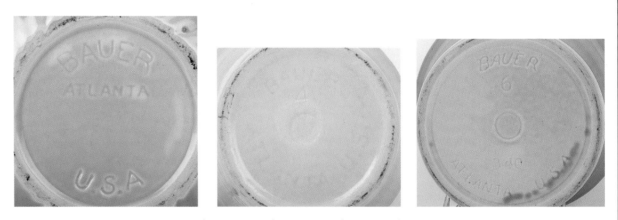

Bauer Atlanta USA marks. *Courtesy of Naomi's of San Francisco.*

Bauer Los Angeles mark. *Courtesy of Naomi's of San Francisco.*

Bauer Los Angeles Made In USA mark. *Courtesy of Naomi's of San Francisco.*

Bauer plain ware divided plate, Delph Blue, 10.5". NP. (**N**o **P**rice) *Courtesy of Naomi's of San Francisco.*

Plain ware plates by Bauer: Orange, 9". $95; Yellow, 7". $75; Blue, 6". $35. *Courtesy of Naomi's of San Francisco.*

Bauer plain ware salad bowl, Delph Blue, 9" diameter. NP. Divided vegetable bowl, Orange, 9.5" diameter. NP—this is an extremely rare item. *Courtesy of Naomi's of San Francisco.*

Bauer plain ware cup and saucer sets. Cup, 2" high, saucer, 6.25" diameter. Red, Blue. $85 set. *Courtesy of Naomi's of San Francisco.*

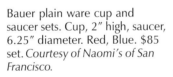

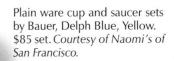

Plain ware cup and saucer sets by Bauer, Delph Blue, Yellow. $85 set. *Courtesy of Naomi's of San Francisco.*

Plain ware Bauer sherbet, Yellow, 2.75". $145. *Courtesy of Naomi's of San Francisco.*

Plain ware pudding bowls by Bauer. Yellow, 7.75" diameter. $65. Green, 5". $45. *Courtesy of Naomi's of San Francisco.*

Ring ware plate by Bauer, 9.25" diameter. Rare "Papaya" color. Cup and saucer set, cup 2.75" high, saucer, 6" diameter. 1941-1945. NP. *Courtesy of Naomi's of San Francisco.*

Two basic colors in Bauer's ring ware: Burgundy and Delph Blue dinner plates, 10.75" diameter. $145-185. *Courtesy of Naomi's of San Francisco.*

Ring ware in two rare colors by Bauer: Black and White platters. $295. *Courtesy of Naomi's of San Francisco.*

Ring ware 10" plate, White. $200+. Black 9" plate. $95+. White 6" plate. $95+. Black 6" plate. $45. Rare White 5" plate. $125. *Courtesy of Naomi's of San Francisco.*

Ring ware platters by Bauer: Brown, 14.5″ diameter. $595; Burgundy, 13″ diameter. $265. *Courtesy of Naomi's of San Francisco.*

Large Bauer ring ware platter, Royal Blue, 17″. $375. *Courtesy of Naomi's of San Francisco.*

Bauer's ring ware chop plates: Black, 17". $1200+; White, 14". $425;
Black, 12". $325+. *Courtesy of Naomi's of San Francisco.*

Berry dish, Delph Blue, 4.25" diameter. $40. Fruit dish, Cobalt, 5.25" diameter. $55. Cereal bowl, Ivory, 5" diameter. $95. Back: Bread and butter plate, Yellow, 5" diameter. $95. Bread and butter plate, Green, 6" diameter. $10. Salad plate, Orange, 7.75" diameter. $30. Plate, Cobalt, 9.25" diameter. $40. *Courtesy of Naomi's of San Francisco.*

Ring ware salad bowls by Bauer: Black, 14" diameter. $425+; White, 12" diameter. $325+; Black, 9" diameter. $225+. *Courtesy of Naomi's of San Francisco.*

Ring ware gravy boat with attached undertray by Bauer, Burgundy. 2.75" high x 7.25" wide. $195. *Courtesy of Naomi's of San Francisco.*

Ring ware sherbet by Bauer, Cobalt, 2.5" high. $95. *Courtesy of Naomi's of San Francisco.*

Ring ware pedestal bowl by Bauer, Green. 7.5" high x 14" diameter. NP. *Courtesy of Naomi's of San Francisco.*

Bauer's ring ware egg cup, Orange, 3.25" high. $295. *Courtesy of Naomi's of San Francisco.*

Ring ware tumblers by Bauer. 12 oz. in Cobalt, 4.5" high. $55. 4 oz. in Jade Green, 3.5" high. $30. *Courtesy of Naomi's of San Francisco.*

Ring ware tumbler assortment by Bauer. Used with or without the handles into which the tumblers may be fit. 12 oz. tumbler, Royal Blue, 4.5" high. $55. 6 oz. tumbler, Jade Green, 3.5" high. $30. 3 oz. tumbler, Yellow, 2.5" high. $95. 6 oz. tumbler, with flared sides, Burgundy, 3.5" high. $65. *Courtesy of Naomi's of San Francisco.*

Bauer ring ware goblet, Orange, 4.5" high. $175. *Courtesy of Naomi's of San Francisco.*

Coffee set, ring ware, by Bauer. Coffee pot, Delph Blue, 8" high. $1400+ (rare shape). Mugs, 4" high. Green, Blue, and Orange. $285. Black. $750. *Courtesy of Naomi's of San Francisco.*

Jumbo Cups by Bauer, ring ware, Cobalt and Delph Blue, 3.25" high x 3.75" diameter. $275. *Courtesy of Naomi's of San Francisco.*

Beer stein, ring ware, by Bauer, Black, 5.25" high. $550. *Courtesy of Naomi's of San Francisco.*

Bauer tea set, ring ware. Teapot, Cobalt, 6" high at lid knob. $265. Standard cream and sugar service, Yellow. Front: Cup and saucer sets in Blue and Yellow, cup 3" high and saucer 6" diameter. $45-60 set. *Courtesy of Naomi's of San Francisco.*

Small Bauer teapot, ring ware, Green, 4.25" high. $245. Cream and sugar caddy, Ivory, 3" high. $495/set (rare color) and $145 more for stand. *Courtesy of Naomi's of San Francisco.*

Standard ring ware cream and sugar service by Bauer. Royal Blue. Pitcher, 3.25" high, sugar bowl, 4" at lid knob. $225/set. *Courtesy of Naomi's of San Francisco.*

Bauer introduced a Family cream and sugar service after the standard design was produced in ring ware. The differences are shown here with this Yellow example. The spout on the pitcher has been elongated and the sugar bowl lid sits on top of the rim, not inside it like the standard set. Family set. $265. *Courtesy of Naomi's of San Francisco.*

One-pint ring creamer (commonly known as a syrup pitcher) by Bauer, Burgundy, 5.5" high at lip. $450. *Courtesy of Naomi's of San Francisco.*

Bauer's ring ware snubnose coffee pot, Orange, 7.5" at lid knob. $245. 8-cup coffee server with wooden handle, from the 1935 California Exposition, 9", Green. $495. Coffee server with metal handle, Cobalt, 8.5" high. $225. *Courtesy of Naomi's of San Francisco.*

8-cup ring ware coffee server by Bauer with wooden handle, Green. $495. 6-cup coffee server with wooden handle, White. $450. *Courtesy of Naomi's of San Francisco.*

Bauer ring ware coffee server with metal handle, 8.5" high. Cobalt. $225. Jade Green. $195. Yellow. $195. Orange. $145. *Courtesy of Naomi's of San Francisco.*

Bauer ring ware coffee servers with metal handle, 8.5" high. Black and White. $395 each. *Courtesy of Naomi's of San Francisco.*

Ring ware ice lip pitcher by Bauer, 7" high to lip. $350. *Courtesy of Naomi's of San Francisco.*

Rare Yellow ring ware ball pitcher by Bauer, 5" high to lip. $695-850. *Courtesy of Naomi's of San Francisco.*

Bauer ring ware butter dish, Maroon. 3.25" high x 6.5" diameter (plate). $275. *Courtesy of Naomi's of San Francisco.*

Bauer ring ware marmalade, Orange, 3" high at lid knob. $450. *Courtesy of Naomi's of San Francisco.*

Salt and pepper shakers, ring ware, by Bauer, Cobalt, 2" high. Salt and pepper shakers, Green and Yellow, 3.5" high. $25 to $55 for shakers. *Courtesy of Naomi's of San Francisco.*

Bauer ring ware sugar shaker, Orange, 5.25" high. $350. *Courtesy of Naomi's of San Francisco.*

Bauer ring ware water carafes with lids (lids are very rare). 9" high. Black. $1600+. Orange. $800+. Delph Blue (no lid). $300. Yellow. $800+. *Courtesy of Naomi's of San Francisco.*

Bauer custard cups, ring ware design. 2.5" high with more flare to the rim than the Hi-Fire line. $16.50 each. *Courtesy of Naomi's of San Francisco.*

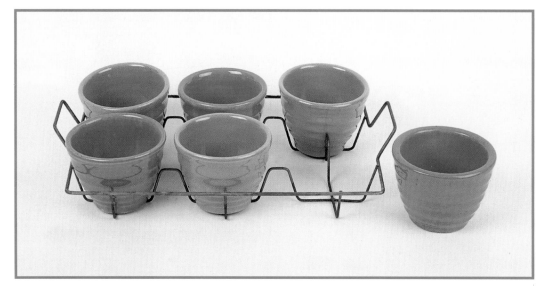

Set of custard cups from Bauer's later Hi-Fire line. Cups, 2.5" high x 3.5" diameter. Orange. $16.50 each. Delph Blue. $55 each. Rack, 11" long x 7" wide. $95. *Courtesy of Naomi's of San Francisco.*

Standard Bauer ring ware pitchers in Orange. 3-quart, 7.25" high to lip. $225. 2-quart, 6.5" to lip $175. 1-quart, 5.5" to lip. $125. 1 1/2-pint, 4.25" to lip. $95. *Courtesy of Naomi's of San Francisco.*

Punch bowls (three footed), ring ware, by Bauer, measuring 9.25" ($350), 11.5" ($600), & 14.5" diameter ($900) respectively. *Courtesy of Naomi's of San Francisco.*

Bauer ring ware mixing bowls. Grey #9, 6" high x 11" diameter. $145. Spruce #12, 5" high x 9.5" diameter. $95. Cobalt #18, 4.5" high x 8" diameter. $65. Yellow #30, 3.5" high x 7" diameter. $40. Orange #36, 3" high x 6" diameter. $30. Note: bowl #24 is missing. This is supposed to be a set of six nesting mixing bowls. bowls made in the 1940s are slightly larger than their predecessors. This is a mixture of both earlier and later bowls. *Courtesy of Naomi's of San Francisco.*

Bauer ring ware cookie jars, 9.5" high at lid knob.
Spruce. $650+. Blue. $750+. Black. $1800+. Yellow.
$650+. *Courtesy of Naomi's of San Francisco.*

Bauer ring ware Spice Jars with lids. Green,
6" high x 8" diameter. $450. Orange, 4.5"
high x 6" diameter. $350. Yellow, 3.5" high x
4.5" diameter. $295. *Courtesy of Naomi's of
San Francisco.*

Ring ware kitchenwares. Left: 2-quart batter bowl; right: rare 1-quart batter bowl (note 2-qt. did not have a lid while the 1-qt. bowl's lid is missing) by Bauer. 4.25" & 3.25" high to lip respectively. $195 for 2-qt.; $350 for 1-qt. *Courtesy of Naomi's of San Francisco.*

Bauer ring ware beater bowl, 1-quart, Green, 5.25". $45. *Courtesy of Naomi's of San Francisco.*

Bauer ring ware beater pitcher, 1-quart, Black, 5" high. $450+. *Courtesy of Naomi's of San Francisco.*

Pickle dish No. 97 by Bauer, Delph Blue, 2" high x 7" long. $65. *Courtesy of Naomi's of San Francisco.*

Bauer nut dish, Redwood Brown, c. 1940s, 3.5" diameter. $25. *Courtesy of Naomi's of San Francisco.*

Bauer plain ware spice jar, Green, 6" high x 7.75" diameter. $450. *Courtesy of Naomi's of San Francisco.*

Plain ware mixing bowl by Bauer, Green, 11".
$195. *Courtesy of Naomi's of San Francisco.*

Bauer plain ware coffee servers, 9.5" high, Orange and
Yellow. $85. *Courtesy of Naomi's of San Francisco.*

Bauer's Gloss Pastel Kitchenware line (1940s) teapot, Brown, 5" high x 11" long. $155. Teapot, pink, 5.5" high x 12" long. $250. *Courtesy of Naomi's of San Francisco.*

Bauer's Gloss Pastel Kitchenware Cookie Jar, 1940s, Chartreuse, 9" high. $125. The Gloss Pastel Kitchenware line was produced by Ray Murray. *Courtesy of Naomi's of San Francisco.*

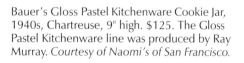

Beater pitcher by Bauer, Dark Brown, 5.25" high. $65. *Courtesy of Naomi's of San Francisco.*

Ashtrays by Bauer: plain ware square ashtray, Yellow, 4". $115. Round ashtray, Orange, 4". $95. Four ashtrays with stand, trays 3", stand 4.25" high. $295/set. The square ashtrays in the stand are from the plain ware line. *Courtesy of Naomi's of San Francisco.*

Monterey line (sometimes referred to as "separated ring ware") by Bauer. Front, Old-style teapot, 6.25" high at lid knob. $135. Back: Serving plate, 13". Orange. $75. Brown. $45. Yellow. $30 (wear). *Courtesy of Naomi's of San Francisco.*

Monterey line by Bauer. 3-footed fruit bowls. Yellow, 13". $225. Burgundy, 10" diameter. $195. Turquoise, 8" diameter. $95. *Courtesy of Naomi's of San Francisco.*

Monterey line by Bauer. Salad bowl, Monterey Brown, 11.5" diameter. $75. *Courtesy of Naomi's of San Francisco.*

Monterey line by Bauer. Tumbler, Burgundy. 4". $15. *Courtesy of Naomi's of San Francisco.*

Monterey line by Bauer, 1936. Coffee pots, Orange and Yellow, 9" high at lid knob. $125. *Courtesy of Naomi's of San Francisco.*

Monterey line by Bauer. Candlestick, Turquoise, 4.25" high. $65. *Courtesy of Naomi's of San Francisco.*

Monterey line by Bauer. Covered refrigerator beverage dispenser, Turquoise, 6.5" high at handle. $300+. *Courtesy of Naomi's of San Francisco.*

Square bowls by Matt Carlton. Top to Bottom: Green, 5" wide. $125. Orange, 7" wide. $195. Green, 9" wide. $225. *Courtesy of Naomi's of San Francisco.*

Matt Carlton refreshment set, Orange. Pitcher, 11". Mugs (should be 6), 4". Tray, 15.75", slightly convex. $1850+ for this rare set. *Courtesy of Naomi's of San Francisco.*

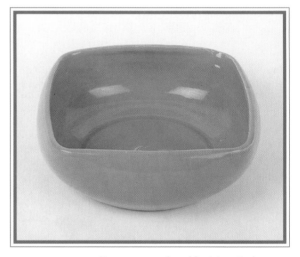

Bauer square bowl by Matt Carlton, Green, 7" wide. $195. *Courtesy of Naomi's of San Francisco.*

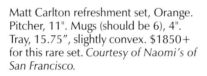

Hi-Fire cylinder vases by Bauer. White, 10.5" high. $195. Blue, 8.25" high. $145. Yellow, 6" high. $125. *Courtesy of Naomi's of San Francisco.*

Bauer oil jars. (Note: 95% were produced in the 16" medium size, 4% in the 22" large size, and 1% in the small 12" size.) Yellow, 12.25". $1200+. White, 16". $2000+. Black (# 124), 20" high $2200+. *Courtesy of Naomi's of San Francisco.*

Bauer oil jars. Delph Blue, 20". $550+. Black (# 129), 24"
$2600+. *Courtesy of Naomi's of San Francisco.*

Rebekah vases by Bauer. Black, 22".
$2200+. White, 20". $2000+. *Courtesy*
of Naomi's of San Francisco.

Rebekah vases by Bauer. White, 18". $1800+. Black,
14". $1400+. White, 12". $1200+. *Courtesy of*
Naomi's of San Francisco.

Rebekah vases by Bauer. White, 8". $800+. Black, 12". $1200+. White, 10". $1000+. *Courtesy of Naomi's of San Francisco.*

Twist handle urns by Bauer. Rare White, Pinched, 10". $1400+. Black, 10". $1000+. White, 8". $800+. *Courtesy of Naomi's of San Francisco.*

Twist-handle (or backward-handled) urns by Bauer. Orange, 18". $1800+. Green, 16" high. $1600+. *Courtesy of Naomi's of San Francisco.*

Bauer Vases. Wavy lip design by Matt Carlton. White, 14". $800+. Black, 12". $495+. Orange, 8". $325+. Green, 6". $250+. *Courtesy of Naomi's of San Francisco.*

Bauer Vases. Wide, wavy lip design by Matt Carlton. Blue, 7.5" high x 10" diameter. $450+. Yellow, 6" high x 11.5" diameter. $450+. Green bowl, 3.5" high x 6" diameter. $95. *Courtesy of Naomi's of San Francisco.*

Matt Carlton vase, Yellow, 6". $225+.
Courtesy of Naomi's of San Francisco.

Matt Carlton Dutch pitchers: White, 11". $850+; Black, 11". $850+. *Courtesy of Naomi's of San Francisco.*

Matt Carlton fan vases. Front: Orange, 6.5" high. $185+. Yellow, 6.25" high. $185+. Orange, 6". $185+. Back: Black, 8" high. $695+ (rare). Blue, 6" high. $200+. Blue, 6" high. $200+. *Courtesy of Naomi's of San Francisco.*

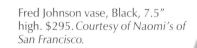
Fred Johnson vase, Black, 7.5"
high. $295. *Courtesy of Naomi's of
San Francisco.*

Fred Johnson vases, 5.25" high. Blue.
$85. White. $85. *Courtesy of Naomi's
of San Francisco.*

Bauer vases: Black, 6" high. $450+;
Black pineapple vase, 5.75" high. $450.
Courtesy of Naomi's of San Francisco.

Matt Carlton floor vase, Blue, 18". $900+.
Courtesy of Naomi's of San Francisco.

Matt Carlton floor vases. Green, 24". $1200. White, 20". $2000. Black, 24". $1200.
Courtesy of Naomi's of San Francisco.

Bauer vases. White 12" vase. $600+; Delph Blue 16" vase. $800+. *Courtesy of Naomi's of San Francisco.*

Bauer umbrella stand or sand jar, Yellow, 20". $395. *Courtesy of Naomi's of San Francisco.*

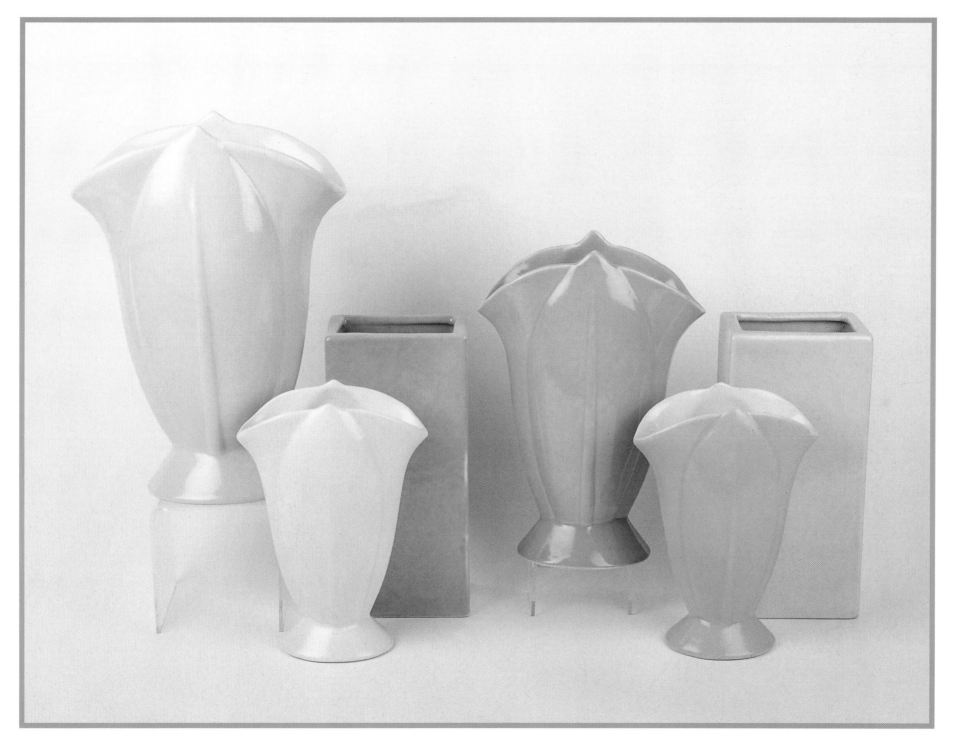

Bauer vase produced in Atlanta, Georgia, 7" high. $95. *Courtesy of Naomi's of San Francisco.*

Bauer Spanish flower pot, Light Blue, 4.25" high. $65. *Courtesy of Naomi's of San Francisco.*

Bauer Spanish flower pot, Light Green, 7.5" high. $85. *Courtesy of Naomi's of San Francisco.*

Bauer lamp, Yellow, base 3.75" high. $695.
Candle holder, Green, 4" high. $595. Lamp,
Green, 3.25" high. $695. *Courtesy of Naomi's
of San Francisco.*

Bauer lamp, Green, base 14"
high. $1600. *Courtesy of Naomi's
of San Francisco.*

Bauer lamp, Black, base 6.5" high. $895.
Courtesy of Naomi's of San Francisco.

Footed lamp by Bauer, Green, 18″ high. $2400. Note: this is an experimental lamp, possibly one of a kind. *Courtesy of Naomi's of San Francisco.*

Bauer lamp, Yellow and Orange, 12″ high. $900. *Courtesy of Naomi's of San Francisco.*

Flower pots by Bauer. Blue, 7" high
$295. Orange, 6" high. $225.
Courtesy of Naomi's of San Francisco.

Bauer flower pots. Yellow, 12" high. $395. Delph Blue, 9" high drilled.
$295. *Courtesy of Naomi's of San Francisco.*

Bauer Indian jars. White, 7" high x 11" diameter.
$1200. Black, 5.75" high x 9.5" diameter. $995.
Courtesy of Naomi's of San Francisco.

Bauer Indian jars, Jade Green. 2.5" high x
4" diameter. $595. 3.5" high x 6" diameter.
$695. 7" high x 11" diameter. $1200.
Courtesy of Naomi's of San Francisco.

Bauer Indian jar. Lavender, a rare color.
9" high x 13.5" diameter. $2400.
Courtesy of Naomi's of San Francisco.

CATALINA CLAY PRODUCTS

Catalina Clay Products was the brainchild of William Wrigley, Jr. and David Renton. The pottery was founded on Santa Catalina Island, owned by Wrigley, in 1927. Renton managed the plant. The pottery's first product was tile. By 1929, the company branched out, producing candle holders, flower bowls, lamps, vases, and a range of decorative souvenirs from the island.

Prior to 1932, at the insistence of William Wrigley, Jr., all of the Catalina ceramics were produced from a local brown-burning clay. This was a problem for the company as the local clay tended to be fragile. Wrigley's death in 1932 allowed for the importation of a more durable white-burning clay from Lincoln, California. Company employees Harold Johnson and Virgil Haldeman are credited with creating the vibrant, original glazes from native island oxides which have long attracted collectors' attentions. Glaze colors produced included Catalina blue, Descanso green, Mandarin yellow, Manchu yellow, Monterey brown, pearly white, sea foam, Toyon red, and turquoise. Later additions to the glaze palate included beige, colonial yellow, coral island, and powder blue in semi-matte finishes.

Catalina turned to the production of tablewares in the early 1930s. Three dinnerware lines were produced, using all of the pottery's glazes. A number of serving pieces were also introduced. In 1936, a new service with a raised rope border motif was added to the line, glazed in satin-finish pastel colors.

Despite the company's successes, in 1937 the pottery was sold to Gladding, McBean and Company, a mainland competitor. In the end, the importation of mainland clay, which improved the Catalina product considerably, also drove up business costs to the point where the sale to Gladding, McBean was necessary. (Chipman 1999, 70-71)

Typical Catalina Marks

Catalina Island mark. *Courtesy of Naomi's of San Francisco.*

Catalina Island Pottery mark. *Courtesy of Naomi's of San Francisco.*

Catalina printed mark. *Courtesy of Naomi's of San Francisco.*

Catalina Island Pottery Moorish design plates, c. 1932, Blue and White, White is much thicker than Blue, 11.25". $350. *Courtesy of Naomi's of San Francisco.*

A dinner place setting in the rare "Monterey Brown" by Catalina Island Pottery. Plate, 11" diameter. NP. Plate, 8.25". $70. Plate, 6". $45. Cup and saucer, cup 2" high, saucer 5.75" diameter. NP. Tumbler, 4.25" high. $68. *Courtesy of Naomi's of San Francisco.*

Opposite page: Catalina Island Pottery dinner plates in Catalina Blue, Mandarin (or Colonial) Yellow, and Toyon Red, 11". $65 each. Match and pipe souvenir holder in Catalina Blue, 7.25" wide. $425. Ashtray in Blue, 6.5" diameter. $95. Coffee cup and saucer, cup 2.25" high, saucer 6.25" diameter. $28 set. Teacup (note the difference) also in Yellow, 2.5" high. $32. *Courtesy of Naomi's of San Francisco.*

Opposite page: Catalina Island Pottery wares. Coffee pot, Blue, 10.25" high. $225. Covered jar, Blue, 5.25" high at lid knob. $325. Vase, Red, 5". $120. Cream and sugar service, Green, pitcher 2", sugar bowl 3" high at lid knob. $145/set. Salt and pepper shakers: Red figural, approx. 4" high. $225/set. Yellow corn, 3.25" high at tallest. $42/ *each* (according to tag). Cabbage-head-type shakers, dark Red ($70), Light Blue, Yellow, and Red, 2.5" high. $42 each. Small round bullet-type shakers, Green and Red. $42 each. *Courtesy of Naomi's of San Francisco.*

Tumblers by Catalina Island Pottery in various colors: Red with handle, Red, Monterey Brown ($68), Yellow ($58), Green ($68), Light Blue, Blue, Seafoam ($68), White ($48), 4" high. ($45-70). *Courtesy of Naomi's of San Francisco.*

Catalina Island Pottery mugs. Brown, Catalina Blue, Toyon Red. 5". $165. *Courtesy of Naomi's of San Francisco.*

Cat "lina" vase (mainland, inkstamp marked, 1937), 4" high x 7.5" wide. $250. Casserole ("Catalina Isle," 1927-1937), 4.25" high at lid knob x 10 1/4 tab to tab. $250. Tab handled bowls (El Rancho pattern, mainland): Green, footed, 6.5" diameter tab to tab x 2" high. Red, 6.75" diameter tab to tab x 2.25" high. $42. Yellow, 7" diameter tab to tab x 2.25" high. Note slight variations. *Courtesy of Naomi's of San Francisco.*

Bottom left: The compote's three pieces: bowl, ring, and glass bowl. *Courtesy of Naomi's of San.Francisco.*

Bottom right: Catalina Island Pottery compote (an icer for shrimp cocktails). Turquoise. 4" high assembled. $165. *Courtesy of Naomi's of San Francisco.*

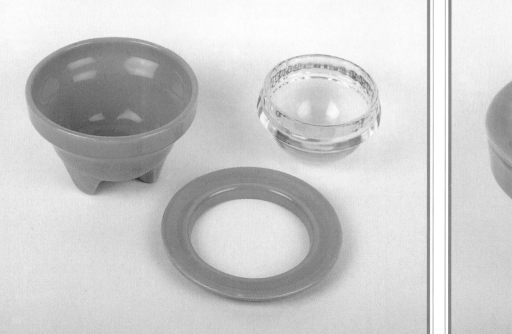

Hand-painted Catalina Island Pottery platter, complete with an artist's signature. 14" diameter. $450. *Courtesy of Naomi's of San Francisco.*

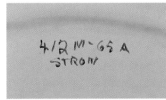

Artist's signature. *Courtesy of Naomi's of San Francisco.*

Hand-painted Catalina Island Pottery piece, no signature. 12.5" diameter. $650. *Courtesy of Naomi's of San Francisco.*

Catalina Island pieces made after Gladding, McBean & Company purchased the Catalina Island Pottery. Ornamental bowls. Fish, White with Blue interior. 5.5" high x 11.5" long. $235. Shell, White with pink interior. 6.5" high x 15" long. $235. *Courtesy of Naomi's of San Francisco.*

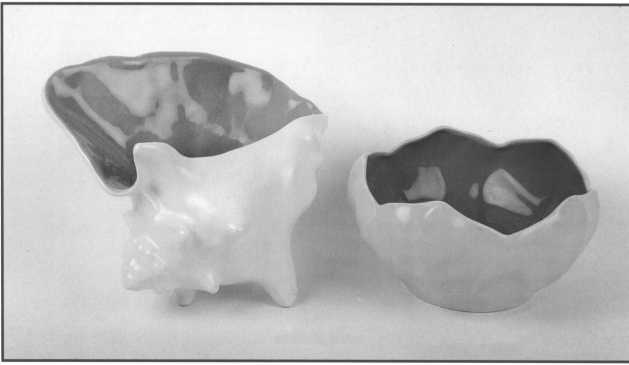

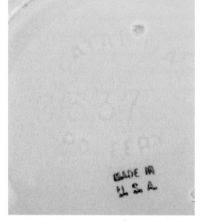

Catalina Island mark, following purchase by Gladding, McBean. *Courtesy of Naomi's of San Francisco.*

Ornamental bowls by Catalina Island Pottery, produced after the company was purchased by Gladding, McBean. Shell, White with pink interior. 6.75" high x 8.5" long. $175. Flower, pink with Blue interior, 4" high x 7.5" diameter. $65. *Courtesy of Naomi's of San Francisco.*

FULPER POTTERY COMPANY

Moving to the East coast, Abraham Fulper purchased the pottery firm of Samuel Hill in Flemington, New Jersey in 1858. At this time, the company produced the usual line of utilitarian stonewares and earthenwares as well as drainage tiles. Abraham's grandson, William Fulper II, took control of the company in the early 1900s, producing artwares with a variety of impressive glazes. William Fulper II produced the Vasekraft art pottery line in 1909.

Fulper pottery tends to be substantial, even heavy. The clay is similar to stoneware but was referred to as earthenware to prevent associating the artwares with utilitarian wares typically produced from stonewares. The clay used by the company was gathered locally from around Trenton. Usually, Fulper pottery was molded, although hand thrown wares were produced for special orders or exhibitions.

Fulper pottery was distinctive for its early use of glaze as the single defining decorative element of the pottery. This shift in decorative technique was startling to consumers familiar with the delicately painted art pottery produced by Rookwood, Roseville, and Weller.

Of the company's glazes, there were over one hundred available at any time, although roughly thirty were most commonly used. Fulper glazes fell into several general categories: mirror, flambe, lustre, matte, wisteria, and crystalline or crystal. Glaze combinations were mixed freely as well. A great number of the glaze colors could be referred to as "earth tones" or "organic."

Fulper Pottery offered a wide range of wares including bookends, bowls, candleholders, desk accessories, figurines, flower frogs, lamps, potpourri jars, and vases. The company introduced a line of green glazed dinnerware to the public in 1920 and added additional glaze colors in 1930. Fulper purchased the Anchor Pottery Company of Trenton, New Jersey in 1926 and transferred most of the company's operations to that plant. This was fortunate as most of the Flemington plant structures were destroyed by fire in 1929. Still, art pottery continued to be produced at Flemington until 1935. (Richey 1999, 38-45)

Typical Fulper Marks

Mark, Fulper. *Courtesy of Naomi's of San Francisco.*

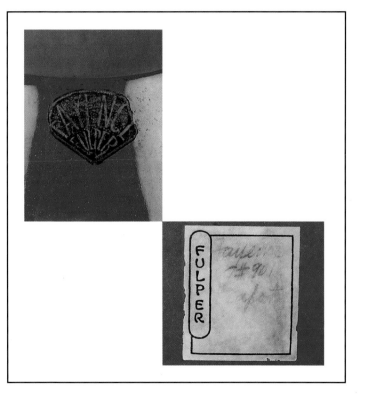

"Fayence" tea set by Fulper Pottery Company including the teapot, trivet, creamer and sugar. Teapot and trivet, Blue, pot 6" high at lid handle, trivet, 6.25" across. Cream and sugar service, Blue, sugar bowl, 3.75" high at lid handle, pitcher, 3.5" high at spout. Teacup and saucer, cup 2" high, saucer, 6.5" diameter. Not shown are the tea cups, saucers and 7" plates that complete this set. $995/set. *Courtesy of Naomi's of San Francisco.*

Fulper handled jug, 6.5". $565.
Hourglass vase, 4.5" high. $225.
Pedestal ball vase, 7.25" high. $295.
Bullet vase, Blue, 6.75" high. $325.
Courtesy of Naomi's of San Francisco.

GLADDING, MCBEAN & COMPANY

In 1875, Charles Gladding, Peter McBean, and George Chambers discovered clay deposits in Placer County, California, and promptly established the firm of Gladding, McBean & Company in the town of Lincoln to manufacture sewer pipe for industries west of the Mississippi. In 1923, Gladding, McBean bought Tropico Potteries, Inc. in Glendale, California.

In 1928, Dr. Andrew Malinovsky improved upon a formula the company had recently purchased, creating a talc earthenware body the company dubbed "Malinite." In 1932, experiments were performed at the Lincoln plant to create dining services and art wares using the new malinite body material, wares which would be decorated with solid-color glazes. This experimentation followed the trend among California potteries: firms which had been producing building materials were beginning to make tablewares for the growing California market.

In 1933, the company purchased the American Encaustic Tiling Company, gaining access to two tunnel kilns capable of firing ceramics at relatively low temperatures. These kilns enabled Gladding, McBean to fire their malinite body and glaze together in a single step. The single firing process fused the glaze with the malinite body, dramatically reducing chances of glaze crazing. The company was now poised to successfully compete in the tableware market.

Fredrick J. Grant, chemical engineer and former president of Weller Pottery in Zanesville, Ohio, was hired in 1934 to manage the new pottery department established at the Glendale plant. His challenge to create complete lines of tablewares, kitchenwares, and artwares using the new malinite body and the single fire process. Grant turned to his wife Mary to develop the style for a new "Franciscan Pottery" line. An art director herself, Mary K. Grant produced many enduring patterns over the years. She was not, however, placed on company payroll until 1938.

Gladding, McBean & Company introduced Franciscan Pottery to the American public in 1934. For the next fifty years, popular, colorful ceramic tablewares of modern design called "Franciscan" were produced in Glendale, California. Over the years, the firm produced close to 150 earthenware patterns and over 185 china patterns. These wares took the forms of dining services, kitchenware, and decorative pieces. The most popular patterns in the Franciscan line were embossed, hand-painted designs created in the 1940s and known as Apple, Dessert Rose, and Ivy.

Mary K. Grant designed the first Franciscan dinnerware pattern, El Patio, produced in August of 1934. El Patio place settings were available in six solid colors and were accompanied by casserole dishes and mixing bowls. Gladding, McBean's solid-color patterns were generally produced in a single color, although two-tone patterns were also produced. El Patio was made in 20 different solid-colors and over 103 shapes. Cups and bowl handles have a distinctive pretzel-like shape. A short-

Gladding, McBean impressive solid-color carafe, tray, and eight cups. Carafe, 8" high. Tray, 16" diameter. Cups, 3.75" high. $395/set. *Courtesy of Naomi's of San Francisco.*

lived variation on the pattern is El Patio Nuevo, manufactured in a two-tone pattern from 1935 to 1936. Interiors and exteriors were given different solid-colors. El Patio was the first Franciscan dining service line produced.

Coronado, another well known solid-color pattern, was produced in the 1930s (c. 1936). Also called Swirl by some for the spiraling shape molded into the pottery, Coronado was decorated in both satin matte and glossy glazes.

By 1939, Gladding, McBean had fifteen patterns in the Franciscan dinnerware line and nine in their artware line. During 1939, the company also developed embossed and hand-painted underglaze patterns which would give them their most popular patterns during the 1940s. In 1940, the company introduced its first embossed and painted pattern, Apple. Around 1941, the firm added Desert Rose to the line. In 1942, Gladding, McBean created Wild Flower, which proved to be their most labor intensive embossed and painted pattern.

Embossed patterns had decorative shapes embossed into the ceramics. These raised shapes were then hand-painted to complete the decoration prior to glazing. The popular and enduring Apple pattern featured bright red fruit, brown branches, and glossy green leaves. All the lids have apple finials.

The Desert Rose pattern featured pink wild roses, light brown thorny branches, and green leaves. The finials on the lids are in shape of rose buds.

As previously mentioned, in 1937 Gladding, McBean and Company had purchased Catalina Clay Products. Gladding, McBean would continue to produce Catalina pottery until around 1942.

As with many American potteries, Gladding, McBean and Company found the later decades of the twentieth century difficult. Despite the popularity of the Franciscan lines over the years, economic recession and foreign competition proved too much for the firm. After a series of mergers and sales, the company was closed in 1984. (Snyder 1996, 8-11)

Typical Gladding, McBean & Company Marks

Gladding, McBean & Company "GMcB" mark. The first mark used by Gladding, McBean & Company when they began their foray into dining services in 1934 incorporated the company initials GMcB inside of an oval. This mark came in two sizes and appeaRed with or without the phrase "Made in USA." This oval mark was found on the solid-color carafe set. The first *Franciscan* mark used was a large capital F placed within a single or double lined box. This replaced the *GMcB* oval mark in September of 1938 and was in use until February 1939. *Courtesy of Naomi's of San Francisco.*

El Patio, the first Franciscan dining service line produced, came in a variety of solid colors and was introduced in 1934. El Patio, Aqua matte finish, 6.75" diameter plate. $9-11; 10.5" diameter plate. $20-22; sugar bowl and creamer. $24-26 set. Note the unique handle shape.

El Patio, Coral glossy finish 10.5" diameter plate. $20-22; 6.25" diameter plate. $9-11; cup and saucer. $20-24.

Coronado pattern White matte finish, coffee pot, NP; 10" diameter plate. $15-19; cup and saucer, $20-24; and cream soup and saucer, $26+.

Coronado is a well-known solid color pattern introduced c. 1936. Coronado pattern (sometimes called "Swirl"), Aqua matte finish, 10.5" diameter plate. $15-19; 8" diameter plate. $9-11; vase, 5.5" high, NP; cup and saucer. $20-24; gravy boat with attached undertray. $30-33; and ashtray. NP.

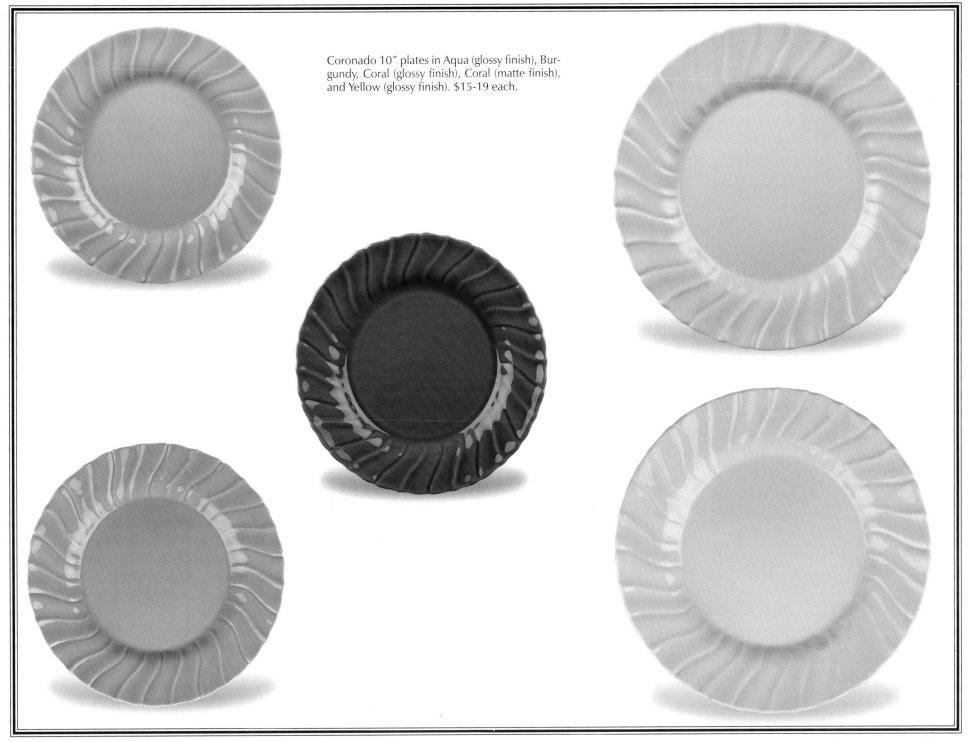

Coronado 10" plates in Aqua (glossy finish), Burgundy, Coral (glossy finish), Coral (matte finish), and Yellow (glossy finish). $15-19 each.

The Metropolitan pattern was designed by Morris Sanders and introduced to the public in 1940. Metropolitan Grey 10″ diameter plate. $15-19; cup and saucer. $20-24; and cream soup bowl and saucer. $26+.

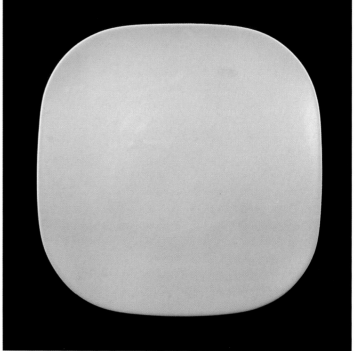

Metropolitan Grey 10″ diameter plate. $15-19.

Apple chop plate, 12.5" diameter, made in America from 1940 onward. $40-44.

Apple individual ashtray, 4.5" long. $22-24.

Apple was the first embossed, hand-painted pattern, introduced by Gladding, McBean on January 1, 1940. Apple place setting and apple shaped salt and pepper shakers, made in America (the English continue to produce this pattern today, but that is well outside of our period of interest). 10" diameter plate, $20-22; 8" diameter plate, $15-17; 6" diameter plate, $8-10; cup and saucer, $11-13; shakers, $23-25 set.

By early 1942, Apple was followed by the embossed, hand-painted pattern Desert Rose. Desert Rose five piece place setting. 10" diameter plate, $18-20; 8" diameter plate, $13-15; 6" diameter plate, $7-9; cup and saucer. $16-18.

Desert Rose 10" diameter plate. $18-20.

Desert Rose chop plate, 12" diameter, $55-60; gravy boat, $35-40; and covered butter dish, $40-45.

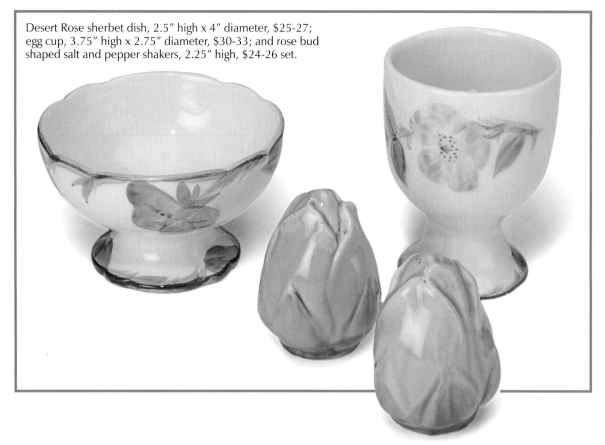

Desert Rose sherbet dish, 2.5" high x 4" diameter, $25-27; egg cup, 3.75" high x 2.75" diameter, $30-33; and rose bud shaped salt and pepper shakers, 2.25" high, $24-26 set.

Desert Rose individual ashtray, 3.5" diameter. $20-22.

Desert Rose oval divided ashtray, 9" long. $60-65.

Desert Rose jumbo cup and saucer. Cup: 4.5" diameter x 3" high, saucer: 7" diameter. $50-55 set.

HALL CHINA COMPANY

The Hall China Company of East Liverpool, Ohio, was founded by Robert Hall in 1903. After an initial foray into both dinnerware and toilet seats, Hall turned to institutional wares for greater profits. By 1904, Robert Hall was dead and the company passed to his son, Robert Taggert Hall.

Robert Taggert Hall found his company's wares prone to crazing. For seven years he experimented until he successfully developed a single fire process allowing both the body and glaze to be fired as one. The process fuses the glaze into the body, reducing the chance of future crazing. Glazes produced by the firm were bright and varied; approximately forty-seven different glaze colors were employed.

With the new process in place, Hall ventured first into table and kitchenwares for hotels and restaurants. An early attempt prior to 1920 to enter the household market with Hall ceramics failed. However, in 1920 the company did succeed in drawing the domestic consumers with a range of decorated teapots. The initial offering came from Hall's institutional line: their Boston, French, and New York teapots adorned with gold decoration.

By 1930, Hall would expand the teapot lines significantly, adding new shapes and colors. While many of the company's utilitarian teapot shapes carried the names of American cities or states, the teapot shapes that really drew consumer attention in those Depression years were the Aladdin and the Rhythm. In the late 1930s, Hall hit a creative high with their unusual and limited novelty teapot line. These novelty teapots would, in fact, be the forerunners of the Pop Art teapots of the 1960s. Hall's halcyon days with their teapot lines ended simultaneously with the Depression years. Demand for the company's creative teapot designs ebbed in the 1940s and 1950s.

When thinking of Hall dinnerware, collectors think first of the Autumn Leaf line, produced exclusively by Hall for the Jewel Tea Company. The Hall China Company began its lucrative association with the Jewel Tea Company of Barrington, Illinois, by providing the firm with teapots to use as premiums. Jewel Tea provided a shop at home service for mid-western housewives, bringing groceries and household or farm products to their doors on a weekly basis. However, Hall would truly profit from the relationship when Jewel Tea needed an exclusive line of dinner and kitchenware to peddle.

This line featured a simple decal decoration and was introduced in the 1930s. When first introduced by Jewel Tea, the line was nameless. By World War II, the pattern was known as "Autumn;" by 1969 the name of the line was "Autumn Leaf." Over the years Autumn Leaf (to use the name most familiar to collectors) would become a very profitable, salable dinnerware line.

French teapots were first introduced by Hall China Company early in the 1920s. The Poppy pattern adorns these examples. Yellow 12-cup ($175), Pink 10-cup ($85), Cobalt 8-cup ($165), Cobalt 6-cup ($125), Light Blue 4-cup ($60), Cobalt 2-cup ($135). 7.25" to 4" high. *Courtesy of Naomi's of San Francisco.*

While several individual pieces of Autumn Leaf were offered in the early 1930s, the first tableware service, a 24 piece breakfast set, was offered in 1936. By 1938, many pieces were sold as open stock directly by Hall. Attesting to the popularity of the line, a complete line of Autumn Leaf dinnerware was being offered by the beginning of World War II. New pieces for this popular line, born in the depths of the Depression, would continue to be produced by Hall for Jewel Tea until 1980.

Additional dinnerware patterns produced by Hall during the Depression include Crocus and Silhouette. From tea to table to storage, Hall produced wares for a variety of purposes and a number of specific companies. By the late 1930s, the electric refrigerator was a very popular device. Rising along with the refrigerator's popularity was the need for convenient cold storage containers. The basic types of storage containers produced by Hall for their refrigerator line included covered butter containers, leftover or refrigerator boxes, and water bottles or water servers. A number of distinctively designed containers were produced as premiums by Hall specifically for individual companies such as General Electric, Hotpoint, Montgomery Ward, Sears and Westinghouse.

Collectors should be aware that the Hall China Company reissued a variety of wares originally introduced in both the 1930s and the 1940s. The reissued wares were part of a "New American" line sold in department stores in the mid-1980s. Reissued items include Airflow and Rhythm teapots, Donut and Streamline jugs, and several water servers. While they were produced with a modern rectangular backstamp and new glaze colors, collectors need to be cautious. (Burns 1996, 1, 41 & 43; Whitmyer 1989, 11-13, 17)

Football novelty teapot by Hall (introduced in 1938), Blue, 6.75" high. $550. *Courtesy of Naomi's of San Francisco.*

Hall China Company teapots. Airflow teapot, (introduced in 1940/this example is a modern example reissued after 1968 only), Yellow, 7.25" high at handle, $115. Teapot, 3-piece, Rhythm (introduced in 1939), 6" high at handle, $265. *Courtesy of Naomi's of San Francisco.*

Autumn Leaf dinner set by the Hall China Company, produced for Jewel Tea. 10", 9", 7", and 6.25" diameter plates (introduced in 1938), and a cup and saucer (introduced in 1936). 10" plate, $14; 9" plate, $9; 7" plate, $8; 6.25" plate, $3.50; cup and saucer set, $9.50. *Courtesy of Naomi's of San Francisco.*

Crocus pattern dinnerware by Hall, introduced in the mid-1930s. 9" plate, $20; 8" plate, $18; 7.25" plate, $18; cup and saucer, $25. *Courtesy of Naomi's of San Francisco.*

Hall's Silhouette pattern "five band" coffee pot, 7.5" high at lid knob. $125. *Courtesy of Naomi's of San Francisco.*

Additional examples of Hall dinnerware patterns. Mount Vernon (blue wreath), 1940s. The largest plate measures 10" in diameter. NP. *Courtesy of Naomi's of San Francisco.*

Pastel Tulip by Hall, early 1940s. 9" plate, $12.50; cup and saucer, $10.50; fruit bowl, $8.50. *Courtesy of Naomi's of San Francisco.*

Springtime by Hall, early 1940s. 10" plate, $10; 7" plate, $8.50; cup and saucer, $10.50; gravy, $16.50. *Courtesy of Naomi's of San Francisco.*

Hall's leftover refrigerator ware produced for Hotpoint. Leftover, round, Maroon, 3.5" high x 7.75" diameter. $75. Leftover, square, Yellow, 3.75" high x 7" wide. $65. Small leftover, square, Orange, 3" high x 4" wide. $42. *Courtesy of Naomi's of San Francisco.*

Typical Hall Marks

Courtesy of Naomi's of San Francisco.

Mark, Jewel Tea.
*Courtesy of
Naomi's of San
Francisco.*

Hall China/Westinghouse mark. *Courtesy
of Naomi's of San Francisco.*

Hall China/Montgomery Ward
mark. *Courtesy of Naomi's of
San Francisco.*

Hall China/Hotpoint
mark. *Courtesy of
Naomi's of San Francisco.*

Hall China/Coldspot mark.
*Courtesy of Naomi's of San
Francisco.*

Hall's Streamline teapot, (introduced in 1937), Red,
6.5" high at handle. $450. New York teapot, Crocus
pattern, 5.5" high at lid knob. $175. *Courtesy of
Naomi's of San Francisco.*

Hall teapots: Streamline teapot, (introduced in 1937), 6.5" high at handle. $350. Hook cover teapot, (introduced in 1940), Cobalt, 5.75" high at handle. $165. *Courtesy of Naomi's of San Francisco.*

Below: Hall made tea sets for Lipton, 1932-1939. In 1932 Hall made a Maroon set for Lipton shops with no cream and sugar. After 1932, Hall produced sets in Light Yellow, Warm Yellow, Light Blue, Black, Green, and Cobalt. Teapot, Green, made for Lipton, 5.75" high at lid handle. $195 (for rare color: other colors usually $50). Cream and sugar service, made for Lipton, pitcher 3" high at spout, sugar bowl 3.5" high at lid knob. $50/set. *Courtesy of Naomi's of San Francisco.*

Windshield teapot, (introduced in 1941), Yellow, 6.25" high. $125. Indiana teapot, (collectors find Indiana difficult to obtain), Ivory, 5.5" high at lid handle. $225. Basket teapot, (a novelty teapot introduced in 1938), Yellow, 6.75" high at handle. $120. Star teapot, (introduced in 1939), Blue with stars, 6.25" high. $95. *Courtesy of Naomi's of San Francisco.*

Airflow teapot, (introduced in 1940), Red, 7" high at handle. $225. Melody teapot, (introduced in 1939), 6.5" high at lid knob. $345. *Courtesy of Naomi's of San Francisco.*

Left: Melody teapot, (introduced in 1939), 6.25" high at lid knob. $395. Right: Surfside teapot, (introduced in 1937), Green, 7.25" high at handle top. $245. *Courtesy of Naomi's of San Francisco.*

Nautilus teapot, (introduced in 1939), 7" high. $225. *Courtesy of Naomi's of San Francisco.*

Aladdin teapot (introduced in 1939), Maroon, 7" high at lid knob. $225. Tea for Two set (the sloping teapot tops differ from a similar Hall Twin-Tee set which have straight tops and were introduced in 1926). This Tea for Two set is a modern example. *Courtesy of Naomi's of San Francisco.*

Hall/Bacharach mark. *Courtesy of Naomi's of San Francisco.*

Sundial teapot, Blue, 7" high at lid handle. $85. *Courtesy of Naomi's of San Francisco.*

T-Ball teapots were produced by Hall for Bacharach of New York around 1948. It is often informative to see wares that either precede or postdate the period of interest. Both teapots have side pockets capable of holding a tea bag each. Left: square, 4.75" high, NP. Right: round, 5" high at lid knob. $145. *Courtesy of Naomi's of San Francisco.*

Automobile novelty teapot (introduced in 1938); Black, 4.25" high x 9" wide. $500. Automobile, teal, 4.25" high x 9" wide. $500+. *Courtesy of Naomi's of San Francisco.*

Forman Family 4 "Adjusto Tea Pot" with two compartments. White. 7.25" high at handle. $75. *Courtesy of Naomi's of San Francisco.*

Top left: Autumn Leaf pattern wares by the Hall China Company, produced for Jewel Tea. Back row: coffee pot with a rayed body (introduced c. 1934), covered marmalade (introduced in 1938), and long spout tea pot with a rayed body (introduced in 1935). Front row: coffee mug (a late conic mug that slipped into this photo, introduced in 1966); and a covered sugar and creamer with rayed bodies (introduced in 1934). Coffee, 8.75" high, $60; marmalade, 4.75" high with 6" diameter underplate, $90; long spout teapot, 8.25" high, $95. Front row: mug, 3.25" diameter x 3.75" high; sugar, 4.5" high & creamer, 4" high to lip, $95 set. *Courtesy of Naomi's of San Francisco.*

Autumn Leaf pattern wares. Back row: platter (introduced in 1938). Front row: open oval bowl (introduced in 1939), gravy boat with underplate (the gravy boat was introduced in 1940; the underplate was first offered in 1942), and covered dish (introduced in 1940). Back row: platter: 13.75" long, $32. Front row: open oval bowl: 10.25" long, $45; gravy boat: 9" long (lip to handle tip) x 3" high to lip, $24; underplate: 8.75" long, $24; covered dish: 5.25" high x 11.5" long handle to handle, $65. *Courtesy of Naomi's of San Francisco.*

Canister set, Radiance shape, the second kitchenware shape line introduced by Hall, 1933. In production from 1934 to 1936 only. This is a very rare color for this line. Flour, Coffee, Tea, Sugar, 7.75" high. Salt and pepper, 5" high. Rare, NP. *Courtesy of Naomi's of San Francisco.*

FLOUR

SALT

COFFEE

TEA

PEPPER

SUGAR

Beer set. Tankard pitcher, 9.75" high. $225. Mugs, 5" high. $95 each. Complete set, pitcher and 6 mugs. $900. *Courtesy of Naomi's of San Francisco.*

Milk Pitcher from the "Five Band" kitchenware line, Yellow, 5" high. $27. *Courtesy of Naomi's of San Francisco.*

Carafe from the "Five Band" kitchenware line introduced in 1936, Green, 9" high at knob. $325. *Courtesy of Naomi's of San Francisco.*

Two Donut jug water pitchers, refrigerator ware, Red. Left: 7.5" high.
$195. Right: 6.75" high. $165. *Courtesy of Naomi's of San Francisco.*

Ball jug water pitcher, Red, 7.25" high.
$95. *Courtesy of Naomi's of San Francisco.*

Loop handle jug water pitcher, refrigerator ware, Orange, 8" high. $125. Hallboy water pitcher, 6.75" high. $22. *Courtesy of Naomi's of San Francisco.*

Plaza water server, Lavender, introduced in 1938, 6.25" high. $450. Ashtray, Lavender, 3.75" high, NP. The lavender glaze was a failure for the company because of its tendency to drip. *Courtesy of Naomi's of San Francisco.*

General line pitcher, refrigerator ware produced for Westinghouse, provided in 1939 as a Westinghouse refrigerator accessory, Blue, 8" high. $185. Montgomery Ward water server, refrigerator ware offered in the early 1940s, Blue. $85. *Courtesy of Naomi's of San Francisco.*

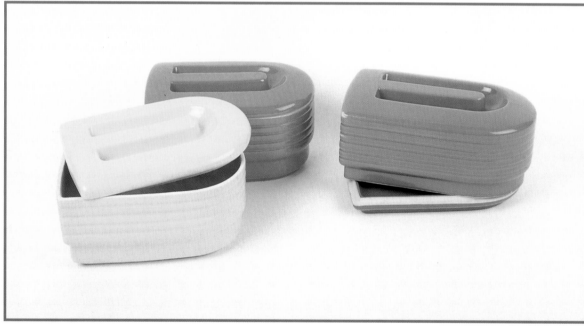

Hercules water server, produced for Westinghouse and available in 1940 and 1941, Cobalt, 9.25" high. $95. Hercules water server with a hinged lid, teal, 9.25" high. $125. *Courtesy of Naomi's of San Francisco.*

General line leftovers and butter dish produced for Westinghouse in 1939. Left: two leftovers: Yellow and Red, 4" high x 6" wide. $45-30. Right: butter dish, 4" high x 6" wide, Green. $65. Be careful how you handle these pieces, knowing where the lid will lift away—leftovers open at the top, butters open at the base. *Courtesy of Naomi's of San Francisco.*

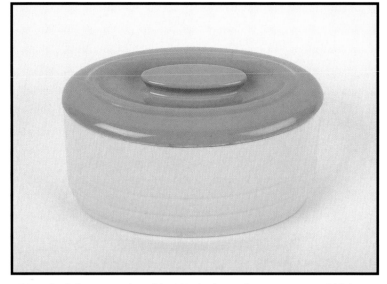

Ridged line casserole, produced for Westinghouse, Yellow, 5.75" high at lid handle by 8.5" long. $45. Ridged line baker, open, Yellow 3" high x 10" wide. *Courtesy of Naomi's of San Francisco.*

Hercules leftover, produced for Westinghouse in 1940-1941, 4" high x 6.5". $45. *Courtesy of Naomi's of San Francisco.*

Phoenix water server, produced for Westinghouse, introduced in 1938, designed for the low shelf in the refrigerator, 5.25" high with lid. $165. *Courtesy of Naomi's of San Francisco.*

For General Electric, Hall adapted the Adonis line refrigerator ware (produced for Westinghouse) to be sold with General Electric refrigerators. Water server, 7" high, missing lid. $75. Leftover, square, 3.5" high x 7" long. $48. Small leftover, round, 2.75" high x 4" diameter. $14.50. *Courtesy of Naomi's of San Francisco.*

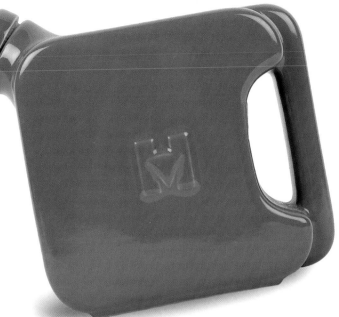

Water server, for Hotpoint, Blue, 7″ high at cork stopper. $150. *Courtesy of Naomi's of San Francisco.*

Montgomery Ward large rectangular leftover, produced in the early 1940s. White, 5.25″ high x 8.5″ long. $125. *Courtesy of Naomi's of San Francisco.*

"Nora" water server, offered as a premium for McCormick, Yellow, 8.75″ high with lid. $125. *Courtesy of Naomi's of San Francisco.*

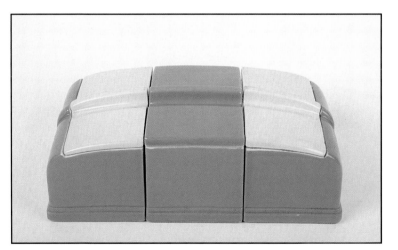

Three compartment leftover set, produced for Sears line. Cadet and Hi-white, 4″ high x 11.5″ long. Complete set. $165. *Courtesy of Naomi's of San Francisco.*

Fiesta is the brightly colored, mass produced, streamlined dinnerware that was first introduced by the Homer Laughlin China Company at the Pittsburgh, Pennsylvania, Pottery and Glass Show of 1936. Introduced during the Depression, the inexpensive, durable, bright Fiesta was much in demand. Fiesta production would continue for decades, until the popular ware was reworked in 1969 as Fiesta Ironstone. Production of Fiesta Ironstone ceased on January 1, 1973.

In 1936, Fiesta was introduced in five solid colors—red, cobalt, light green, yellow, and ivory. Over the years, Fiesta grew to become the most famous product of a prolific china company.

Homer Laughlin and his brother Shakespeare first opened their pottery company in East Liverpool, Ohio, in September of 1874. Shakespeare Laughlin would leave the business to Homer in 1877 to pursue other interests. The Homer Laughlin China Company was incorporated in 1896. This successful business operation expanded across the river to Newell, West Virginia, by 1907 and by 1929 the entire operation had transferred to Newell.

In 1927, the company hired Frederick Hurten Rhead as art director. Rhead was assigned the task of increasing the artistic qualities of the company's wares. In 1935, Fiesta was the grand culmination of Rhead's experiments in shapes and glazes. Rhead designed Fiesta to be durable, bright, and inexpensive. He marketed Fiesta to the working class, which Rhead had calculated to constitute roughly forty percent of the American population during the Depression. Once again, consumers were encouraged to mix-and-match the colorful wares. Rhead had calculated well: Fiesta became the Homer Laughlin China Company's most successful line.

Fiesta has smooth, flowing, streamlined lines and a pleasing concentric circle motif in tune with the Art Deco styling prevalent during the Depression years. The concentric circle design captures some of the colored glaze, creating distinctive, delicate highlights along the circular contours.

However, the colorful glazes are the most arresting feature of Fiesta. Fiesta's white talc body was the perfect surface upon which to display the brilliant red, yellow, cobalt, light green, and ivory originally offered in 1936. A semi-reflective finish was applied, eliminating glittering highlights and focusing the viewer's attention on the colors themselves. Turquoise was added to the Fiesta color spectrum in 1938. The remainder of the eleven colors that would grace Fiesta over the years fall beyond the scope of this book.

In 1986, a new Fiesta line was introduced by the Homer Laughlin China Company to commemorate Fiesta's 50th birthday. This modern Fiesta, with all new glaze colors, and—as of this writing—an ever widening array of wares, proves to be as popular with consumers today as the original Fiesta is with collectors. (Snyder 1999, 11-30)

HLC Fiesta Made in USA mold impressed mark. *Courtesy of Jean E. Newsome, The Antique Shop, West Chester, Pennsylvania.*

Genuine Fiesta HLC USA mark. *Courtesy of Jean E. Newsome, The Antique Shop, West Chester, Pennsylvania.*

A Fiesta montage featuring the original five colors of 1936 (Red, Yellow, Cobalt, Light Green, Ivory), and Turquoise (added in 1937). Fiesta was created by the Homer Laughlin China Company. *Courtesy of Jean E. Newsome, The Antique Shop, West Chester, Pennsylvania.*

Fiesta chop plate in brilliant Red, 14.25" in diameter. $85-95. *Courtesy of Jean E. Newsome, The Antique Shop, West Chester, Pennsylvania.*

Fiesta chop plates: Red, 14.25" diameter, $85-95; Yellow, 12.25" diameter, $40-45. *Courtesy of Jean E. Newsome, The Antique Shop, West Chester, Pennsylvania.*

Fiesta plates by the Homer Laughlin China Company. Turquoise, 10.25" diameter, $40-45; Cobalt, 9.5" diameter, $17-19; Light Green, 7.25" diameter, $7-8; Ivory, 6.25" diameter, $5-6; Cobalt cup and saucer (6" diameter saucer, 3.25" diameter cup), $35-40. *Courtesy of Jean E. Newsome, The Antique Shop, West Chester, Pennsylvania.*

Fiesta Yellow coffee pot, Cobalt and Red cups and saucers, and sugar bowl. (See the following photos for prices.) *Courtesy of Jean E. Newsome, The Antique Shop, West Chester, Pennsylvania.*

Yellow Fiesta coffee pot. $200-225. *Courtesy of Jean E. Newsome, The Antique Shop, West Chester, Pennsylvania.*

Fiesta Red cup and saucer. 6" diameter saucer, 3.25" diameter cup. $39-42. *Courtesy of Jean E. Newsome, The Antique Shop, West Chester, Pennsylvania.*

Light Green Fiesta sugar bowl. 5" high. $60-65. *Courtesy of Jean E. Newsome, The Antique Shop, West Chester, Pennsylvania.*

Fiesta Cobalt disk water pitcher, 7.25" high, 6" high to the lip. $165-180. *Courtesy of Jean E. Newsome, The Antique Shop, West Chester, Pennsylvania.*

Fiesta Cobalt and Yellow disk pitchers. The Yellow disk juice pitcher measures 5.75" high, 4.75" high to the lip. $40-45. *Courtesy of Jean E. Newsome, The Antique Shop, West Chester, Pennsylvania.*

Yellow Fiesta sauce boat. 8.25" long x 4" high to the lip. $45-50. *Courtesy of Jean E. Newsome, The Antique Shop, West Chester, Pennsylvania.*

Three Fiesta tumblers: Cobalt water tumbler, 4.5" high x 3.5" diameter, $85-90; Ivory and Red juice tumblers, 3.5" high x 2.5" diameter. Ivory juice tumbler, $45-50; Red juice tumbler, $45-50. *Courtesy of Jean E. Newsome, The Antique Shop, West Chester, Pennsylvania.*

Fiesta salt and pepper shakers, Cobalt and Yellow. 2.5" high. $15-20 single Cobalt shaker; $10-12 single Yellow shaker. *Courtesy of Jean E. Newsome, The Antique Shop, West Chester, Pennsylvania.*

PACIFIC CLAY PRODUCTS COMPANY

Until recently, the brilliant and appealing pottery from the Pacific Clay Products Company has not been well known outside of the West Coast. The primary plant for the Pacific Clay Products Company was located in the Lincoln Heights district of Los Angeles, California. The company was created in the early 1920s when William Lacy brought together several disparate potteries. The company's early products were focused on supporting California's building boom of the 1920s, including brick, roofing tile, and terra cotta.

Of course, with the Depression came an end to aggressive building projects. Seeking new direction, Pacific followed Bauer's example, entering the new market for colored table and kitchenwares. Pacific brought forth a line of dining and serving pieces christened Hostessware shortly after Bauer introduced its popular California Colored Pottery in 1930. With a greater variety of wares available in the Hostessware line, Pacific's offering gave Bauer stiff competition.

The quality of Pacific's colored wares was high. The company policy was to discard seconds. The streamlined styling and dynamic glaze colors were very appealing to the public. The following glaze colors were first offered: Apache Red, Aqua, Cactus Green, Delphinium Blue, Desert Brown, Jade Green, Lemon Yellow, Pacific Blue (a deep cobalt), and Sierra White. As the years passed, these colors would be altered and given new names.

A startling variation to the single glaze color decoration common to colored dinnerware of the Depression was Pacific's hand painted underglaze decorations which varied in form from simple bands and spirals to more complex patterns.

Artwares were not ignored at Pacific; a variety of pleasing slip-cast artware products were produced during the 1930s. Among these objects were candle holders, figurines, flower bowls and flower frogs, planters, and vases.

World War II brought an end to the Pacific Clay Products Company's promising pottery production as the company contracted with the government and turned its production toward military production. (Chipman 1999, 193-195; Cox 1996, 160-161)

Typical Pacific Marks

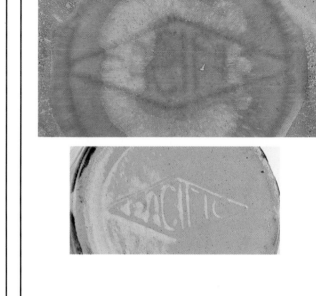

Pacific mark. *Courtesy of Naomi's of San Francisco.*

Pacific Made In USA mark. *Courtesy of Naomi's of San Francisco.*

Pacific Pottery paper label. *Courtesy of Naomi's of San Francisco.*

Divided Pacific relish plates. 9.25"
diameter. $75. *Courtesy of Naomi's of
San Francisco.*

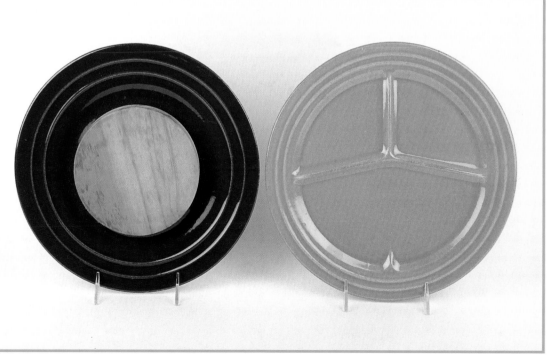

Cheese and cracker plate (#635) with cutting
board, Pacific Blue, 11" diameter. $195.
Divided plate, Apache Red, 11.5" diameter.
$40. *Courtesy of Naomi's of San Francisco.*

Canapé sets, #651 and 652. Left: 2.25" high cup, 7.5" diameter plate. Right: 2.25" diameter cup, 8" diameter plate, with flange. $135—2-piece sets. *Courtesy of Naomi's of San Francisco.*

Pacific bowls. Cream soup bowl, Apache Red, 5 1/2" diameter. $20. Individual #205 baker, 4.5" diameter. $22. Custard (#206), 4" diameter. $16. *Courtesy of Naomi's of San Francisco.*

Pacific salad bowl, Apache Red, 8" wide. $65. Vegetable dish, Apricot, 9.25" wide. $65. Mixing bowl, Apache Red, 7.25" diameter. $58. *Courtesy of Naomi's of San Francisco.*

Sherbets. 3.25" high. $55. *Courtesy of Naomi's of San Francisco.*

Egg cup, 3.5" high. $65. *Courtesy of Naomi's of San Francisco.*

Salt and pepper shakers. 2.25" high. $45/set. *Courtesy of Naomi's of San Francisco.*

Ball pitcher #420, 6.5" high to lip. $125. *Courtesy of Naomi's of San Francisco.*

Coffee carafe with lid (2 qt., #438), Pacific Blue, 9.25" high. $95. Buffet bottle with lid (2 qt.), Delphinium Blue, 8.25" high. $125. *Courtesy of Naomi's of San Francisco.*

Pacific 7-oz. cups in various colors. Back, Left to Right: Pacific Blue, Delphinium Blue, Aqua, Lemon Yellow, Apache Red. Front: Apricot, Sierra White. 4.25" high. $20 each. *Courtesy of Naomi's of San Francisco.*

Pacific 7-oz. #411 coffee mug. Apache Red. (The second cup is not Pacific) 4.25" high. $20. *Courtesy of Naomi's of San Francisco.*

Back, Right to Left: 11-oz cups, 5" high. $55. 11-oz #421 ball tumbler, 5.5" high. $95. 9-oz #419 ball tumblers, 5" high. $35. Front: 11-oz footed goblets, 5.5" high. $85. *Courtesy of Naomi's of San Francisco.*

Large tumblers, #431, 4" high. $65. *Courtesy of Naomi's of San Francisco.*

Teapot (#440, "Art Deco"), 8 cup, Yellow, 5.75" high at lid knob. $165. Coffee pot, 10 cup, very rare, Red, 10" high at lid knob. $300. Teapot (#447), 6 cup, Jade or Cactus Green, 7.5" high at lid knob. $195. Front: Small teapot (#446), 4 cup, Turquoise Blue, 6" high at lid knob. $195. *Courtesy of Naomi's of San Francisco.*

Teacups and saucers. Cup: 2.75" high, saucer: 6" diameter. $35/set (although Pacific Blue and Sierra White glazed items tend to be valued slightly higher than the rest). *Courtesy of Naomi's of San Francisco.*

Coffee cup and saucer, cup 3.25" high, saucer 6" diameter. $35/set. Teacup and saucer, cup 2.75" high, saucer 6" diameter. $22/set. *Courtesy of Naomi's of San Francisco.*

Demitasse cup and saucer. 2.75" high cup, 4.5" diameter saucer. $65 set. *Courtesy of Naomi's of San Francisco.*

Individual cream (#449) and individual sugar bowl (#450). No lid was made for this small, open sugar. 2.75" high. Creamer, Apache Red. $30. Sugar bowl, Apricot. $30. *Courtesy of Naomi's of San Francisco.*

Small pitcher, 3.75" high. $55. Covered baker, 3" high. $40. *Courtesy of Naomi's of San Francisco.*

Pacific bulls eye platter with tab handles (#413), 16" diameter tab to tab. $195. Bulls eye platter (#451), no tabs, 15.75" diameter. $225. *Courtesy of Naomi's of San Francisco.*

"Chip and dip" plate (#661), 11.25" diameter. $95. *Courtesy of Naomi's of San Francisco.*

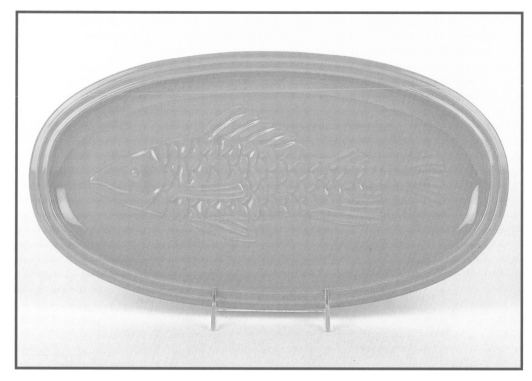

Pacific Fish Platter, 16" wide. $195-225.
Courtesy of Naomi's of San Francisco.

Pacific platter (#444), 14" wide. $125.
Courtesy of Naomi's of San Francisco.

Pacific handled serving dish (#663, a multiple use piece used as either a relish or a bon bon dish), 9.5" wide. $68. *Courtesy of Naomi's of San Francisco.*

Pacific divided vegetable dish (#640), 12" wide x 2.5" high. $75. *Courtesy of Naomi's of San Francisco.*

Pie plate (detachable handles missing), 11" diameter. $75. *Courtesy of Naomi's of San Francisco.*

Pacific open baking bowls in 2 sizes (detachable handles missing). Left: #224, Jade/Cactus Green, 9.75" diameter. $85. Right: #223, Delphinium Blue, 8.75" diameter. $85. *Courtesy of Naomi's of San Francisco.*

Soup tureen #604, footed, 5.5" high x 9.75" diameter. $245. *Courtesy of Naomi's of San Francisco.*

Waffle syrup pitcher (footed), 5.25" high at lid handle. $175. Waffle pitcher (footed), 7.25" high at lid handle. $250+. *Courtesy of Naomi's of San Francisco.*

Pitcher (#429, 1 quart), 5.5" high. $95. Pitcher, 4.5" high. $75. *Courtesy of Naomi's of San Francisco.*

Three branch candlesticks (#707) by Pacific, 3.5" high x 10.5" long. $145/pr. *Courtesy of Naomi's of San Francisco.*

Range set (#232): salt & pepper shakers. Missing is a drip can belonging in center. 4-4.25" high. $125 for shaker pair. *Courtesy of Naomi's of San Francisco.*

Pacific Candle Holders. Bottom: #715 square candlesticks, 3" high. $90/pair. Top: #705, 2" high. $165/pair. *Courtesy of Naomi's of San Francisco.*

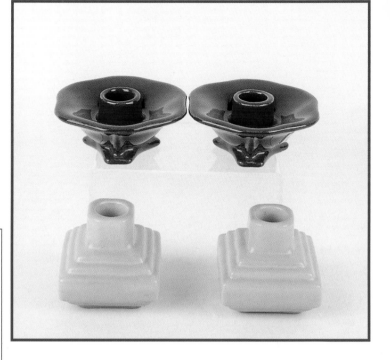

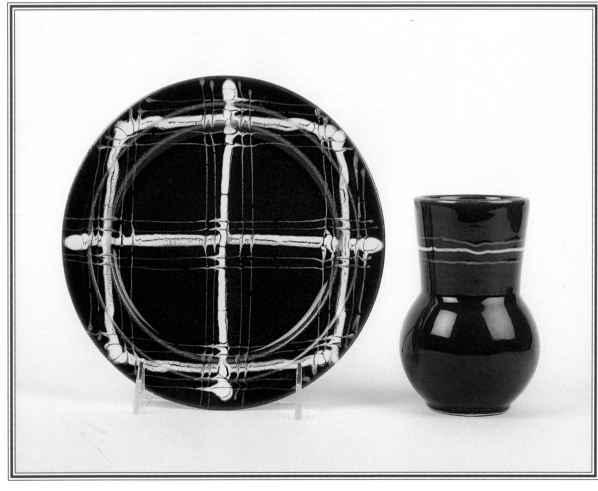

Hand-painted wares. Plate, 7.5" diameter. $45. Vase, 5" high. $65. *Courtesy of Naomi's of San Francisco.*

Artist's initials. *Courtesy of Naomi's of San Francisco.*

Hand-painted wares. Plate, 9.25" high. $95. Plate, 9.25" high. $95. *Courtesy of Naomi's of San Francisco.*

Hand-painted wares, Aqua. Back: Plate, 9.25" diameter. $135. Front: Cream and sugar service, pitcher 2.75" high at rim, sugar bowl 2.75" high at rim. $165 set. Teacup and saucer, teacup 3" high, plate, 6" diameter. $125 set. *Courtesy of Naomi's of San Francisco.*

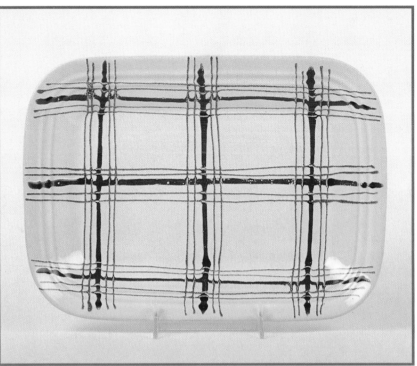

Hand-painted teacup and saucer. Cup, 3" high, saucer, 6" diameter. $125. *Courtesy of Naomi's of San Francisco.*

Rectangular platter, White with plaid design, 9" x 12.75". $225. *Courtesy of Naomi's of San Francisco.*

Hand-painted wares. Teacup and saucer, Yellow, cup 3" high, saucer 6" diameter, $125. Teacup and Saucer, Cobalt, cup 3" high, saucer, 6" diameter, $125. *Courtesy of Naomi's of San Francisco.*

Hand-painted teacups, 3" high. $65. *Courtesy of Naomi's of San Francisco.*

Coffee pot, 9.25" high. $155.
Courtesy of Naomi's of San Francisco.

"Buffet Server" pitcher, without lid, 7" high. $145. *Courtesy of Naomi's of San Francisco.*

Bowl, blended glaze stoneware popular in the late 1920s, 5" high x 10" diameter. $485. Bowl, blended glaze stoneware, 4.75" high x 9.5" diameter. $485. *Courtesy of Naomi's of San Francisco.*

Blended glazed stoneware mugs, #502, popular in the late 1920s, 4.5" high. $165. *Courtesy of Naomi's of San Francisco.*

Large storage jar with lid, blended glaze stoneware, 10.25" high x 12.75". This is a rare mint condition Pacific jar. $1250. *Courtesy of Naomi's of San Francisco.*

Pictured George Washington vases (usually a "George & Martha" pair was sold as a set in matching colors). 5.75" high. $18 each. *Courtesy of Naomi's of San Francisco.*

Large floor vase, Aqua, 25.75" high. $500+. 12.5" high vase, Aqua. $95. *Courtesy of Naomi's of San Francisco.*

Large Pacific vase, Pastel Green, 15.25" high. $400+. *Courtesy of Naomi's of San Francisco.*

Vase, 6.25" high. $45. Vase, 7" high. $65. *Courtesy of Naomi's of San Francisco.*

With Rookwood, the focus is on handsome design and beautiful glazes. As previously stated in the introduction, back in the late 1800s ceramic painting was very popular with the ladies. That passion for ceramic painting led directly to the establishment of Rookwood Pottery, possibly the leading American art pottery, in Cincinnati, Ohio. Rookwood Pottery was founded in 1880 by Maria Longworth Nichols. Maria Nichols worked on her own in a studio over a wagon shed owned by Dallas Pottery of Cincinnati. Shortly thereafter, her father, Joseph Longworth, purchased an old schoolhouse for her, where she set up her own pottery works, naming the new pottery Rookwood. A friend of hers from Dallas Pottery, Joseph Bailey, Sr., assisted in the purchase of equipment and materials for the operation. Joseph Bailey, Sr. also arranged for an outlet to sell the new Rookwood Pottery wares. Mr. Bailey's son, Joseph, Jr., hired on as Rookwood's first employee. Rookwood Pottery was ready for operation in September 1880. (Gilchrist 1981, 116)

Albert Valentien, one time student of the Cincinnati School of Design, was hired to head the decorating department in the fall of 1881. Under his direc-   tion, Rookwood motifs were to use American flora and fauna. (Levin 1988, 70 & 74)

Vases, turned on the potter's wheel, were the most common form produced at the newly established Rookwood Pottery. Rookwood pieces were signed by their designers. In the late nineteenth century, the Rookwood designs were greatly influenced by Japanese design, and the Japanese emphasis on fine glazes. In fact, so taken was Maria Nichols with Japanese design that she hired the Japanese designer, Kataro Shirayamadani, who became Rookwood's most famous artist. Mr. Shirayamadani was particularly well known for the quality of his underglaze painting. Among the many glossy Rookwood glazes of note, the shimmering crystalline Tiger Eye glaze was especially admired. (Gilchrist 1981, 116)

Rookwood candle holders, 1935, 2.75" high. $200+ for pair. *Courtesy of Naomi's of San Francisco.*

In 1901, Rookwood introduced a line of mat glazes, which were very popular with the public at that time. Among their mat glazes were conventional mat, incised mat, modeled mat, painted mat, and painted mat inlay. Leaping ahead, the 1920s would be Rookwood Pottery's final decade of great successes. The Depression years quickly took their toll on Rookwood. One year after the stock market crash of 1929, the company was struggling with its finances. By the end of 1932, the company's decorators were laid off. Several decorators continued to work on special order projects. At this point, decorated wares were curtailed and pieces adorned only with distinctive shapes and glazes were created. Master potter Earl Menzel created a Dip/

Drip line during this period. The lines Coromandel, Later Goldstone, and Later Tiger Eye were all in production during this period as none required decorators. (Ellis 1995, 10)

Rookwood Pottery wares may be divided into the decorated and the commercial wares. Artist decorated wares fall into the first camp and the decorations are unique. The commercial wares, on the other hand, are mass produced, decorated by simpler means, and are not unique objects. With the commercial wares, *art pottery* (frequently hand turned—or hand made—as well as artist decorated) gave way to mass produced commercial *artware*. Included among the commercial wares are objects featuring molded body decorations. (Ellis 1995, 7; Huxford 1995, 15)

Beginning in 1941, mounting financial problems would lead to several sales of the struggling firm. By 1967, the Rookwood Pottery Company was finished.

Typical Rookwood Marks

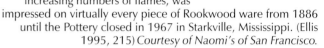

Rookwood mark. The RP logo with no flame was introduced in June 1886. In 1887, a single flame was impressed over the RP logo, and an additional flame was added every year until 1900, when 14 flames surrounded the Rookwood monogram. In 1901, the Roman numeral I was impressed below this trademark and changed accordingly with each additional year. This mark XXIX refers to the year 1929. (This mark was used with the flame(s) from 1887-1967) This mark, with increasing numbers of flames, was impressed on virtually every piece of Rookwood ware from 1886 until the Pottery closed in 1967 in Starkville, Mississippi. (Ellis 1995, 215) *Courtesy of Naomi's of San Francisco.*

Rookwood bowl with flower frog, 1930, 7" diameter. $225. Small bowl, 1930, 4" diameter. $125+. *Courtesy of Naomi's of San Francisco.*

Rookwood bowl, 1936, 3" high x 8.25" diameter. $200+. *Courtesy of Naomi's of San Francisco.*

Rookwood vase, 1929, 6.5" high. $300+. Small Rookwood jug, 1929, 3.75" high. $100+. *Courtesy of Naomi's of San Francisco.*

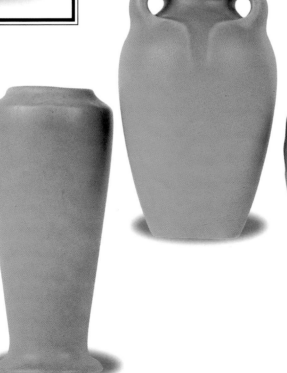

Rookwood vases. Left to right: Vase, 1930, 6.25" high. $125. Vase, 1934, 5.5" high. $300+. Vase, 1930, 5.5" high. $200+. Vase, 1930, 5 1/4" high. $200+. *Courtesy of Naomi's of San Francisco.*

Small Rookwood vase, 1930, 3.75" high. $150. *Courtesy of Naomi's of San Francisco.*

Small Rookwood vase, 1932, 3.75" high. $400+. *Courtesy of Naomi's of San Francisco.*

Rare Rookwood vase with a Reddish Brown micro-crystalline glaze, 1931, 5" high. $300+. *Courtesy of Naomi's of San Francisco.*

Rookwood vases. Vase, 1932, 4.5" high. $300+. Vase, 1934, 5.25" high. $300+. Vase, 1931, 6" high. $200+. Vase, 1934, 4.75" high. $400+. *Courtesy of Naomi's of San Francisco.*

Small Rookwood vase, 1934, 5" high. $300+. *Courtesy of Naomi's of San Francisco.*

Rookwood vase, 1934, 5.5" high. $300+. Vase, 1930, 5.25" high. $300+. Vase, 6" high. $250+. Vase, 1930, 5.25" high. $300+. *Courtesy of Naomi's of San Francisco.*

Rookwood footed vase with dancing women decorating both sides, 1935, 9" high. $400+. *Courtesy of Naomi's of San Francisco.*

Rookwood small vase, 1936, 4.75" high. $200+. *Courtesy of Naomi's of San Francisco.*

Artist-signed Rookwood vases. Left to right: Lorinda Epply, 1930 6.25" high. $1165. Margaret McDonald, 1937, 6" high. $1325. Sally Coyne, 1930, 7.25". $995. Lorinda Epply, 1931, 4" high. $785. *Courtesy of Naomi's of San Francisco.*

Lorinda Epply's mark. *Courtesy of Naomi's of San Francisco.*

Margaret McDonald's mark. *Courtesy of Naomi's of San Francisco.*

Janet Harris's mark. *Courtesy of Naomi's of San Francisco.*

Sally Coyne's mark. *Courtesy of Naomi's of San Francisco.*

Wilhemina Rehm's mark. *Courtesy of Naomi's of San Francisco.*

Mostly Rookwood artist-signed vases. Left to right: Wilhemina Rehm, 1930, 5.75" high. $1095. Janet Harris, 1930, 5.5" high. $965. *Courtesy of Naomi's of San Francisco.*

The Roseville Pottery Company, first established in Roseville, Ohio, in 1890, was acquired by George Frank Young and the company manufacturing was transferred to Zanesville, Ohio, in 1898. The company produced both commercial and art pottery products. By the late 1800s, the company was successful enough to purchase several additional potteries in the area, extending the firm's ability to create a wider range of pottery wares. By 1901, Roseville operated four plants. (Cox 1996, 183; Huxford 1995, 11)

By 1900, George Young believed his company was diverse enough to compete with Weller in the art pottery market. Ross Purdy was hired to develop and launch the company's first art pottery line, Rozane. The Rozane line featured a variety of well executed forms decorated with deep, blended background colors complemented with a variety of natural motifs, including flora and fauna, and portraits. (Huxford 1995, 12)

The success of the initial line led to a wide variety of art lines in the years to come. The continued success of the company propelled it from one modest plant employing 45 workers to a well established competitor producing commercial artware on a very large scale by the outbreak of World War II, with sales exceeding one million dollars. Roseville wares reached consumers through major department stores and catalog houses throughout the nation. Between 1890 and 1954, the prolific Roseville Pottery Company would manufacture some 132 different product lines. Four generations of George Young's family would guide the company over the years until it closed in 1954. (Coleman 1994, 34-37; Bassett 1999)

Roseville lines produced during the Depression years (and slightly before in the case of Futura) include:

Futura (1928), Imperial (1930 glazes), Earlam (1930), Ferella (1930), Sunflower (c. 1930), Montacello (1931), Windsor (1931), Jonquil (ca. 1931), Ivory (1932), Baneda (1932), Blackberry (ca. 1932), Cherry Blossom (1933), Tourmaline (1933), Artcraft (1933), Falline (1933), Wisteria (1933), Laurel (1934), Topeo (1934), Luffa (1934), Russco (1934), Pine Cone (1935—one of the company's most successful lines), Velmoss (1935), Morning Glory (1935), Orian (1935), Clemana (1936), Primrose (1936), Moderne (1936), Moss (1936), Thorn Apple (1937), Dawn (1937), Ixia (1937), Poppy (1938), Teasel (1938), Fuchsia (1938), Iris (1939), Cosmos (1939), Crystal Green (ca. 1939), Bleeding Heart (1940), White Rose (1940), Columbine (1941), Rozane Pattern (1941), Bushberry (1941). (Bassett 1999)

Typical Roseville Marks

Courtesy of Naomi's of San Francisco.

Futura pattern, 1928, by Roseville. Ball vase, Green, 10.25" high. $850+. Square vase, Pink and Green, 8" high. $600+. Ball vase, pink and Green, 8" high. $400+. *Courtesy of Naomi's of San Francisco.*

Futura, 1928. Vase, pink, 8.25" high. $400+. Vase, Blue, 7.75" high. $600+. Vase, Blue, 9.25" high. $450+. *Courtesy of Naomi's of San Francisco.*

Futura, 1928. Front: Bud vase, 6.25" high. $400+. Flower holder with frog, 3.5" high x 12.25" wide, frog fits in tapered bottom. $800+. Back: Vase, 6.25" high. $350+. Vase, pink, 4" high. $350+. bowl, Blue, 3.75" high. $350+. *Courtesy of Naomi's of San Francisco.*

Futura, 1928. Vase, 9" high. $600+. Vase, Blue and Green, 10" high. $600+. *Courtesy of Naomi's of San Francisco.*

Futura, 1928. Jardiniere, 9" high. $400+. Vase, 6.25" high. $250+. *Courtesy of Naomi's of San Francisco.*

Peony, 1930, by Roseville. Mugs, Yellow and Green, 3.75" high. Vase (two-handled), Yellow, 4.25" high. $45. Two-handled bowl, 6.25" high. $195. *Courtesy of Naomi's of San Francisco.*

Sunflower, 1930 by Roseville. Front: Vase, 5.25" high. $500+. Vase, 5.25" high. $400+. Back: Vase, 6.25" high. $700+. Bowl (or wide-mouthed vase), 4" high. $600+. *Courtesy of Naomi's of San Francisco.*

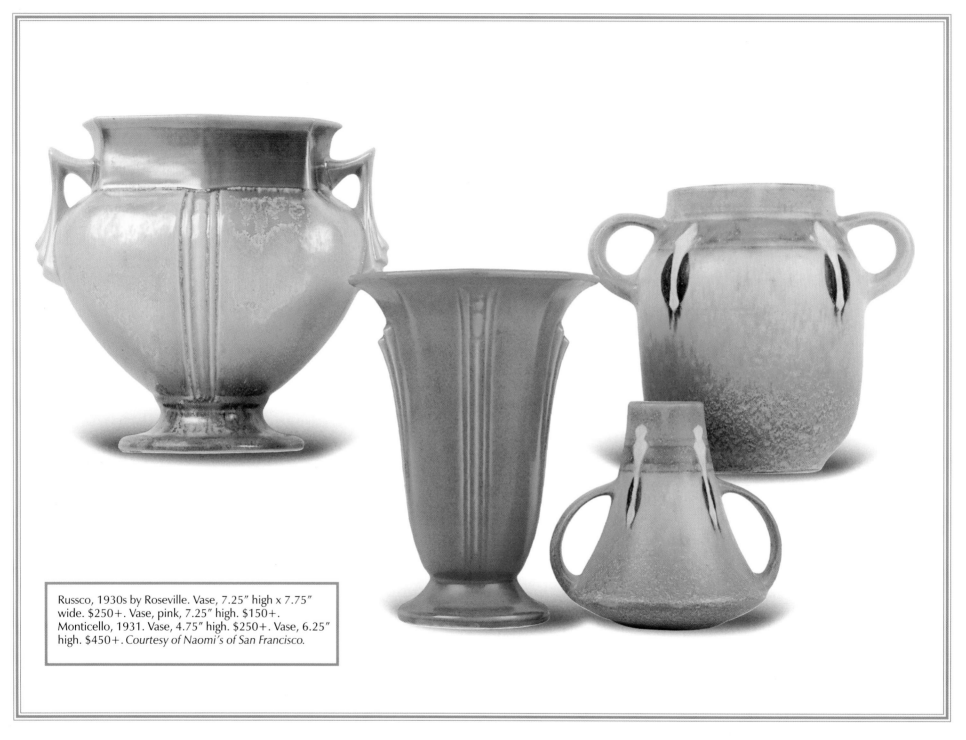

Russco, 1930s by Roseville. Vase, 7.25″ high x 7.75″ wide. $250+. Vase, pink, 7.25″ high. $150+. Monticello, 1931. Vase, 4.75″ high. $250+. Vase, 6.25″ high. $450+. *Courtesy of Naomi's of San Francisco.*

Baneda, 1933, by Roseville. Vase, 4.25" high. $395+. *Courtesy of Naomi's of San Francisco.*

Windsor, 1931, by Roseville. Handled jug, 9.5" high. $800+. *Courtesy of Naomi's of San Francisco.*

Laurel, 1934, by Roseville. Vase, 7.25" high. $450+. *Courtesy of Naomi's of San Francisco.*

Blackberry, 1933, by Roseville. Vase, 6" high. $300+. *Courtesy of Naomi's of San Francisco.*

Wisteria, 1933, by Roseville. Vase, 9.25" high. $450+. Vase, 7.25" high. $450+. *Courtesy of Naomi's of San Francisco.*

Topeo, 1934, by Roseville. Shallow bowl, 4 tabs, 2.75" high x 8" diameter. $225. Shallow bowl, 9" diameter, 6.5" diameter at rim. $225. *Courtesy of Naomi's of San Francisco.*

Morning Glory, 1935. Vase, White, 8.25" high. $500+. Two-handled vase, Green, 4.25". $450+. Cherry Blossom, 1933. Vase, 7.25" high. $250+. Ball vase, 5.25" high. $250+. Hourglass vase, 8.25" high. $275+. *Courtesy of Naomi's of San Francisco.*

Pine Cone bowl, 1935, by Roseville, 2" high x 9" wide. $225. Bowl, 1.5" high x 7" wide. $145.
Courtesy of Naomi's of San Francisco.

Pine Cone mug, 4.25" high. $265.
Courtesy of Naomi's of San Francisco.

Pine Cone candle holders by Roseville, 4.5" high. $465 for pair. Pine Cone bowl, 3.75" high. $245.
Courtesy of Naomi's of San Francisco.

Pine Cone planters. Back left: 4.5" high x 11.5" wide. $450. Back Right: 3.5" high x 9" wide. $265. Front: 3.5" high x 15.75" wide. $425. *Courtesy of Naomi's of San Francisco.*

Blue Pine Cone tray, 2" high x 12.5" wide. $295. *Courtesy of Naomi's of San Francisco.*

Pine Cone vases by Roseville. Left to right: Vase, 8.25" high. $565. Vase, 9.5" high. $425. Vase, 7.25" high. $265. *Courtesy of Naomi's of San Francisco.*

Pine Cone vases: footed vase, 10.5" high. $445. Handled footed vase, 8.25" high. $495. Pedestal vase, 7.25" high. $275. Cornucopia vase 8.25" high. $325. *Courtesy of Naomi's of San Francisco.*

Green Pine Cone vase, 1935, by Roseville. 5.25" high. $145. *Courtesy of Naomi's of San Francisco.*

Bleeding Heart, 1938, by Roseville. Two-handled vase, 4" high. $125. Teasel, 1936. Two-handled vase, 4.75" high. $195. *Courtesy of Naomi's of San Francisco.*

RUSSEL WRIGHT

The pottery designs of Russel Wright work well to lead us out of the Depression pottery years and give collectors a hint of what would come in the following decades. Russel Wright was an industrial designer working with organic designs that featured flowing lines and soft contours. Surrealism appears to have influenced his work. By 1937, Wright had completed the designs for his "American Modern" line. Wright produced the glaze colors for the "American Modern" line with the assistance of the Alfred University ceramics department.

Russel Wright's unusual designs and glaze treatments left many potters reluctant to produce his wares. However, the bankrupt Steubenville Pottery of East Liverpool, Ohio, took on the challenge. In 1939, Russel Wright's dinnerware was first made available to the public. With an aggressive advertising campaign and Wright's innovative approach to salesmanship—introducing the public to the allure of the "starter set"—the American Modern dinnerware line was to become very popular with consumers in years to come. (Levin 1988, 171)

Typical Russel Wright Mark

Russel Wright Mfg. by Steubenville mark. *Courtesy of Naomi's of San Francisco.*

Russel Wright's "American Modern." Seafoam and Chartreuse Curry: teacup and saucer. Bread plate, 6" diameter. $8. Salad plate, 8" diameter. $25. Dinner plate, 10" diameter. $11.50. Square chop plate, 12.5". $75. Note: Seafoam tends to be higher-priced than Chartreuse ... but not always. *Courtesy of Naomi's of San Francisco.*

Produced by Russel Wright for Bauer in the 1940s. Front: Oblong bowl, shape 9A "Canoe", Figured White, 2 /34" high x 23.5" wide. $850-900. Square ashtray, shape 10A, Bubble White on outside, Blue inside, 2.25" high. $300-350. Back: Shape 2A, Figured White, 8" high. $550-600. Planter with undertray, Jonquil Yellow, 7" high together. $550-650/set. Half Egg shape 17A, 2.25" high x 10" wide. $600-800. "Rollover" ashtray (no shape number), Figured White outside and Aqua inside, 2.25" high x 6.5" wide. $725. *Courtesy of Naomi's of San Francisco.*

Opposite page, left: Seafoam and Chartreuse Curry. Teacup and saucer. Bread plate, 6" diameter. $8. Salad plate, 8" diameter. $25. Dinner plate, 10" diameter. $11.50. Square chop plate, 12.5". $75. Note, Seafoam tends to be higher-priced than Chartreuse ... but not always. Low range: Chartreuse Curry, Coral Pink, Granite Gray. Middle range: Seafoam (Cedar Green, Black Chutney). High range: White, Bean Brown, Glacier Blue, Canteloupe. Very Rare: Steubenville Blue. *Courtesy of Naomi's of San Francisco.*

Teacups and saucers demonstrating the spectrum of colors Russel Wright offered in the "American Modern" line of 1939. Seafoam, Chartreuse Curry, Granite Gray, White, Coral, and Bean Brown. The cup measures 2" high and the saucer measures 6" in diameter. Chartreuse, Coral, and Granite Gray cup and saucers sets are valued at $11.50 per set. Seafoam sets are $18 per set. White and Bean Brown sets are worth $35 per set. Wright would introduce other colors as years went by. *Courtesy of Naomi's of San Francisco.*

Celery plate, Chartreuse, 13" long. $30. Salad or Vegetable bowl, Seafoam, 2.5" high, x 10" long. $45. Artichoke platter, Gray, 13.5" long. $35. *Courtesy of Naomi's of San Francisco.*

Large salad or vegetable bowl, Seafoam, 4.25" high x 11" long. $125. *Courtesy of Naomi's of San Francisco.*

Top to bottom: small baker, Coral, 9.75" high to tab. $65. Sauce boat, Gray, 8.75" tab to tab. $65. Lug salad bowl, Seafoam, 7" including tab. $30. Lug fruit bowl, Coral, 6.25" including tab. $20. *Courtesy of Naomi's of San Francisco.*

Divided vegetable dish. Coral, 1.75" high x 13" long. $95. *Courtesy of Naomi's of San Francisco.*

Woodfield serving fork and spoon set, Gray, 10.75" long each. $195/pair. *Courtesy of Naomi's of San Francisco.*

Relish rosette, Seafoam, 11.25" diameter. $345. Salt and pepper shakers, Chartreuse, 2" high. $10.

Gravy boat, Coral, 2.5" high x 10.25" long. $25. Underplate, Chartreuse Curry, 11" long. $25. *Courtesy of Naomi's of San Francisco.*

Individual ramekin, Coral, 2.75" high x 5.5" diameter. $145. *Courtesy of Naomi's of San Francisco.*

Covered baker, Chartreuse, 4" high x 12" diameter (including handle). $45. Covered lug vegetable bowl, Seafoam, 4" high x 12" diameter (including tabs). $75. *Courtesy of Naomi's of San Francisco.*

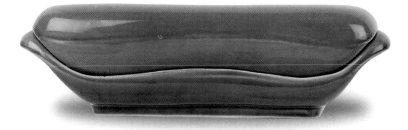

Covered butter dishes, Chartreuse and Seafoam, 8.5" long. $295. *Courtesy of Naomi's of San Francisco.*

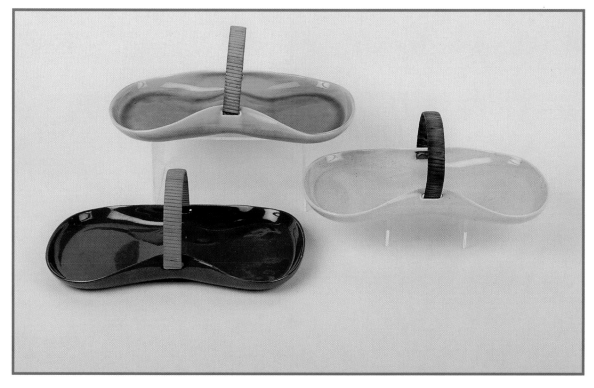

Divided relish, 4.25" high to top of rattan handle x 10.25" long, Chartreuse and Gray. $265. Bean Brown relish. $285. *Courtesy of Naomi's of San Francisco.*

Water pitcher, Seafoam, 10.5" high. $125. Covered pitcher (called an icebox water server), 7.5" high. $295 as is. Wine carafe (missing wood stopper, which is very rare), Coral (two tone—gray inside, coral outside—rare), 6" hish. $325. *Courtesy of Naomi's of San Francisco.*

Wine carafe (missing wood stopper, which is very rare), Coral (two tone—gray inside, coral outside—rare), 6" hish. $325. *Courtesy of Naomi's of San Francisco.*

Tumbler, Chartreuse, 3.5" high. $95.
Coaster, Gray, 3.5" diameter. $45.
Courtesy of Naomi's of San Francisco.

Teapot, Bean Brown, 4.75" high. $195. Cream and sugar service, Coral, 3" high x 7" long. $15. Sugar bowl, Chartreuse, 3.25" high (at handle) x 6.5" long. $25. After-dinner coffee pot, Coral, 4.25" high x 8.5" long. $135. Demitasse cups and saucers, cup 1.4" high, saucer 4" diameter, Chartreuse Curry set, $32; Seafoam set, $45. *Courtesy of Naomi's of San Francisco.*

Coffee pot, 6.75" high. $295.
Courtesy of Naomi's of San Francisco.

Coffee pot, cup and saucer, and a rare coffee cup cover (do not confuse these covers with coasters). The coffee cup cover, in Coral, measures 4" in diameter. NP. *Courtesy of Naomi's of San Francisco.*

Ice box jar, Coral, 2.75" high x 6"
diameter. $120. *Courtesy of
Naomi's of San Francisco.*

Three-piece stack set, Coral, 6.75" high. $365. *Courtesy of Naomi's of San Francisco.*

Samuel A. Weller first established a small pottery in Fultonham, Ohio, in 1872. With early success, Weller was able to move his business to Zanesville, Ohio, a decade later in 1882. Samuel Weller would retain control of his company until his death in 1925, when the firm was passed to his nephew, Harry Weller.

In 1895, Samuel Weller purchased the Lonhuda Pottery of Steubenville, Ohio. With that purchase, Weller also obtained the techniques and means of producing Lonhuda art pottery, an underglaze, slip decorated ware. With that purchase, Weller Pottery launched upon a long career in the art pottery market. The company's first move was to rename the Lonhuda line Louwelsa and rerelease it to the public. Louwelsa, decorated in yellow and brown glazes, would sell well for the company from 1895 to 1918, featuring over five hundred items in the line. (Henzke 1996, 277)

By 1905, the company was competing successfully in the art pottery market. At that time, the company had some twenty different styles available, including Sicardo. Sicardo glaze colors blend with one another, mingling the deep red, vibrant green, and peacock blues. Sicardo forms are elegant art nouveau styles and the vessels are ornamental, including bowls, candlesticks, jewel boxes, and vases. While Sicardo added prestige to the Weller name, it was costly to produce and had a limited run. (Henzke 1996, 278)

Following World War I, the company needed to produce less expensive lines of pottery. At this point the company began producing molded lines. Many of the molded patterns were drawn from American scenes, flora and fauna. One of the lines from this period, "Woodcraft," featured owls and foxes in woodland motifs. The company's "Zona" line, featuring bright red apples on a light colored background, would be sold to Gladding, McBean & Company to become the basis for the popular Franciscan Apple line. (Henzke 1996, 278, 281)

John Lessel, an expert in the use of metallic luster glazes, was hired by Weller as the company's art director in 1920. In this position, Lessel created Lamar, Marengo, and other metallic and luster glazes. He is also credited with perfecting the company's Chinese red Chengtu line. (Henzke 1996, 281)

Dorothy England, one of the firm's modelers, created a number of striking later company patterns including the Ollas Water Bottle. This bottle was shaped as a gourd with a stemmed lid. It was glazed in a variety of colors and had an underplate. (Henzke 1996, 282)

When the Depression began, demand for expensive hand decorated art pottery and commercial artwares diminished. To survive in this difficult market, Weller ceased most of their hand decoration and introduced two new inexpensive single fire lines a year. These lines were distinguished by their glazes alone. The Cactus line was an example of the new, inexpensive line. Cactus animal figurines were molded, glazed and fired once. These lines did well for themselves during the Depression years. Bonito was another inexpensive line, introduced in 1932. (McDonald 1997, 18-21)

Weller also produced a wide range of utilitarian wares to compete in the difficult Depression period market. Light Blue Banded Ware, a white glazed cookware decorated with a wide pinstripe line on either side, was a perfect example of this utilitarian ware. While few house-

Weller Louwelsa vase, c. 1895, 5.75" high. $645. *Courtesy of Naomi's of San Francisco.*

wives were in the market for jardinieres or vases, all would still need casseroles and mixing bowls.

The repeal of Prohibition in 1933 offered Weller another opportunity. The factory produced beer mugs enthusiastically to meet the pent up demand of the previously dry society. (McDonald 1977, 18-21)

Weller Pottery survived the Depression, continued through the war years, but succumbed to financial difficulties and foreign competition in 1948.

Woodcraft bowl (featuring a squirrel), Weller, 1920-1933, 3.25" high x 6.25" wide. $225. *Courtesy of Naomi's of San Francisco.*

Forest pattern vase, dating from the mid-teens through 1928, Weller, 8.25" high. $260. Basket, 3.25" high x 5.75" wide, impressed Weller mark. $295. Bowl, 3.25" high x 6" wide, impressed Weller mark. $165. *Courtesy of Naomi's of San Francisco.*

Weller Lusterware planter, 1920, 7" high. $145. These are difficult to find. *Courtesy of Naomi's of San Francisco.*

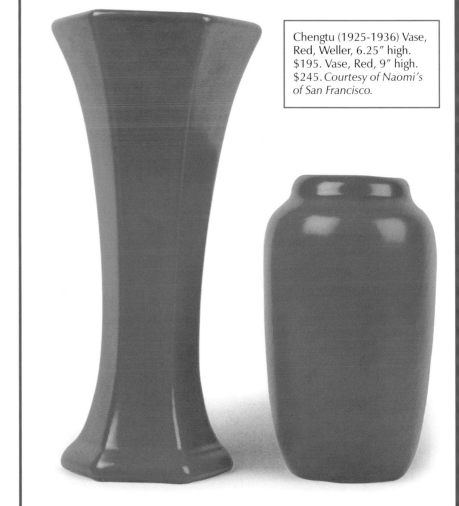

Chengtu (1925-1936) Vase, Red, Weller, 6.25" high. $195. Vase, Red, 9" high. $245. *Courtesy of Naomi's of San Francisco.*

Weller "luster" vase, Orange, 1920, 7.75" high, $165; "lustre" vase, Blue, 10" high, $95. *Courtesy of Naomi's of San Francisco.*

Ollas gourd-shaped water bottle and undertray by Weller dating from the late 1930s. Water bottle, 12" high; tray, 8.25" diameter. $165 for 3-piece set. *Courtesy of Naomi's of San Francisco.*

Teapot, pink, 7.25" high. $95. *Courtesy of Naomi's of San Francisco.*

Teapot, Brown, 6.5" high, impressed Weller mark. $95. *Courtesy of Naomi's of San Francisco.*

Typical Weller Marks

Courtesy of Naomi's of San Francisco.

Weller marks: Weller Pottery since 1872 B-S. *Courtesy of Naomi's of San Francisco.*

Weller Pottery mark. *Courtesy of Naomi's of San Francisco.*

Frog bowl. 10 1/2" w. $465. *Courtesy of Naomi's of San Francisco.*

Groora flower frog, Weller, early 1930s. 4.5". $95. *Courtesy of Naomi's of San Francisco.*

Coppertone flower frogs, Weller, late 1920s. Left: 2.5" high. $75. Right: 2" high. $60 each. *Courtesy of Naomi's of San Francisco.*

Coppertone jardiniere, Weller, late 1920s, 10" high x 12" wide. $1250. Vase, Weller, 6.75" high, hand written mark (in script). $950. *Courtesy of Naomi's of San Francisco.*

Fleron vase, late 1920s, 8.5" high. $325.
Courtesy of Naomi's of San Francisco.

Coppertone pattern by Weller, dating from
the late 1920s. Vase, 8.75" high, and
console bowl, 11.25" diameter. $595.
Courtesy of Naomi's of San Francisco.

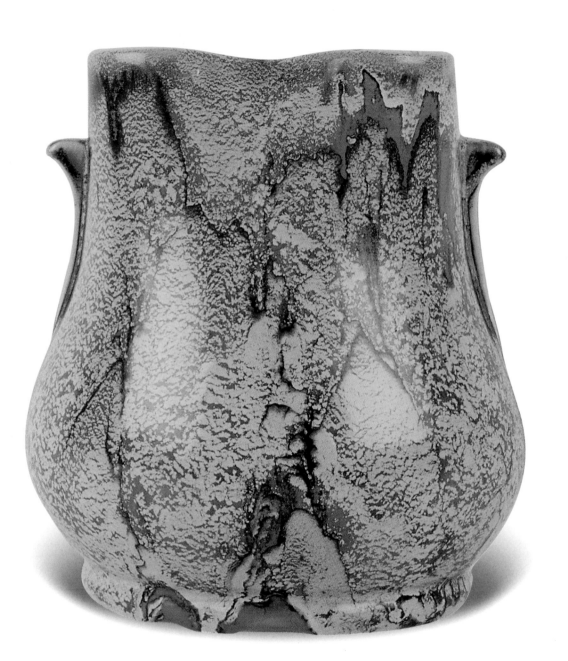

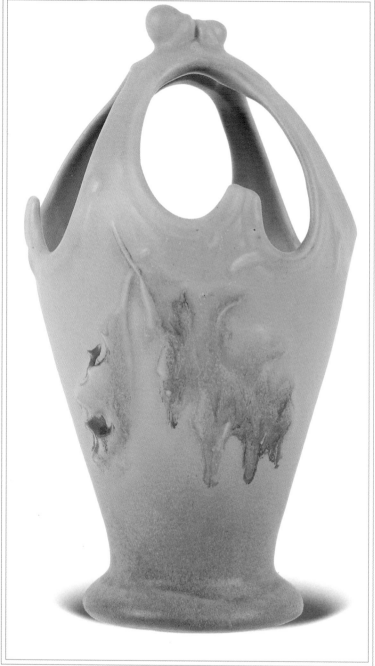

Greenbriar vase, early 1930s, 7.75" high. $395. *Courtesy of Naomi's of San Francisco.*

Oak Leaf basket vase with an impressed (script) Weller mark, dating from before 1936. $95. *Courtesy of Naomi's of San Francisco.*

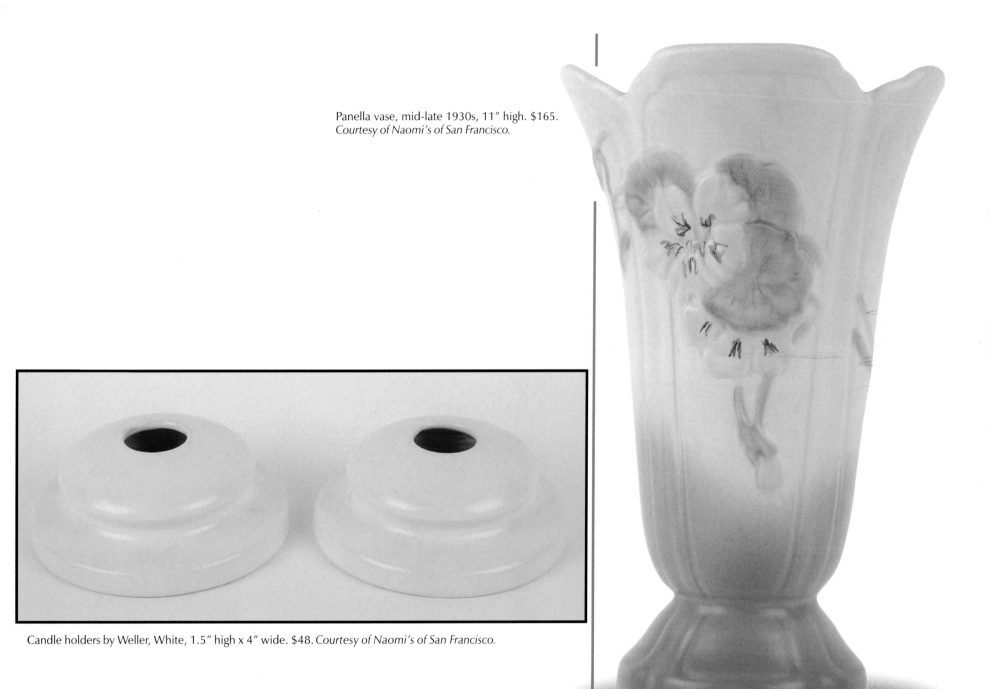

Panella vase, mid-late 1930s, 11" high. $165.
Courtesy of Naomi's of San Francisco.

Candle holders by Weller, White, 1.5" high x 4" wide. $48. *Courtesy of Naomi's of San Francisco.*

Pedestal bowl, Blue, by Weller, 4.25" high, impressed
Weller mark. $75. *Courtesy of Naomi's of San Francisco.*

Softone pitcher dating from the early 1930s to 1935,
9.5" high with an impressed (script) Weller mark. $55.
Courtesy of Naomi's of San Francisco.

Fanciful Weller duck-rabbit-penguin in Yellow & White, 6.25" high. $125 each. *Courtesy of Naomi's of San Francisco.*

Weller duck-rabbit-penguin, Yellow, 6.25" high. *Courtesy of Naomi's of San Francisco.*

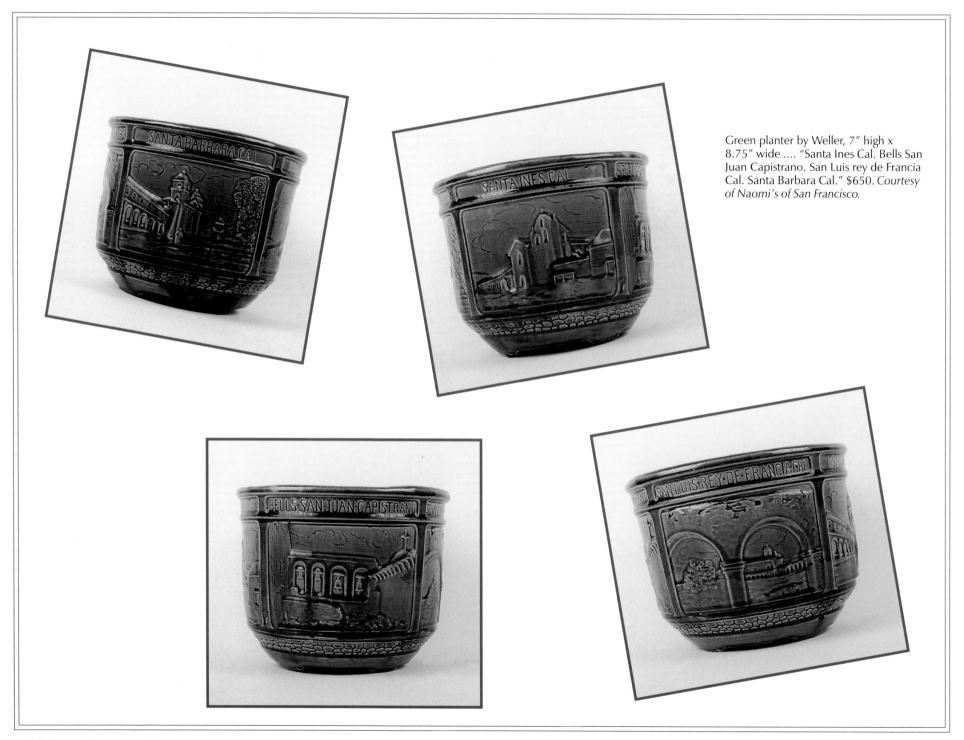

Green planter by Weller, 7" high x 8.75" wide .... "Santa Ines Cal. Bells San Juan Capistrano. San Luis rey de Francia Cal. Santa Barbara Cal." $650. *Courtesy of Naomi's of San Francisco.*

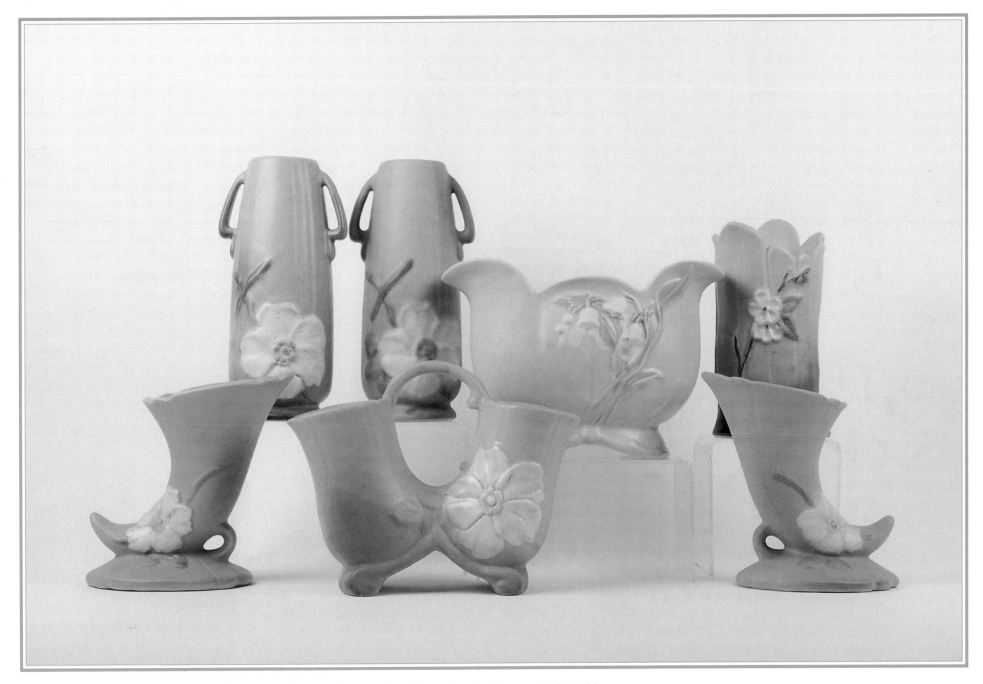

Florist's vases by Weller produced in the early to mid-1930s. All except the wide peach colored vase are in the Wild Rose pattern The wide peach colored vase has the Bouquet pattern produced in the late 1930s. Two Green 8" vases, $85 each; two "cornucopia" 6" vases, $85 each; double vase with handle measuring 6.5" high x 8.5" wide, $125; a wide peach colored 5.75" high x 8.5" wide vase (top row, center), $65; three-leg Green vase, 6.75" high, $95. *Courtesy of Naomi's of San Francisco.*

If you find yourself attracted to the styles, glazes, and techniques popular in pottery during the Depression years, the following potteries should also receive your consideration for their similarity in style. If you find these wares attractive, the challenge will be to find the items themselves!

SOCIALLY MINDED CERAMICS — SATURDAY EVENING GIRLS, PAUL REVERE, AND MARBLEHEAD

The Saturday Evening Girls was a club for young immigrant girls established by Mrs. James J. Storrow of Boston, Massachusetts. The purpose of the group was to help familiarize the new arrivals with Boston and to give them a pleasant place to associate and learn the potting trade. Mrs. Storrow purchased a kiln in 1906 and established the club. In 1908, the club relocated from a Brookline address to an establishment close to the Old North Church. The club's membership grew to include over two hundred young ladies. In time, the expanding group's name was changed to Paul Revere Pottery. Designer Edith Brown became the pottery's director at this point and eliminated amateur potters in favor of high school girls she trained to fill the positions. Children's breakfast sets and dinnerwares decorated with floral designs were produced.

Wares produced by this small enterprise were sold in gift shops and in the pottery's showroom. The company was never truly successful in the financial sense, surviving largely on subsidies from Mrs. Storrow. In 1932, Edith Brown died and the company slowly came undone. Paul Revere was closed in 1942 and Mrs. Storrow passed away in 1944. (Levin 1988, 118; Henzke 1996, 169)

Marblehead Pottery was in business from the early 1900s to 1936. The pottery originated with Dr. Herbert J. Hall, founder of a sanatorium in Marblehead, Massachusetts. Dr. Hall felt that his patients, women suffering from nervous disorders, would be benefited by becoming occupied with simple, manual tasks, such as pottery decoration. In 1905, Dr. Hall hired Arthur Baggs, a ceramics student from Alfred University, to act as the pottery's manager and provide artistic guidance.

Arthur Baggs was interested in making the company a financial success. Soon the company was devoid of patients as decorators and was an independent operation. In 1908, Marblehead Pottery wares were introduced to consumers. Baggs would go further and purchase the pottery in 1915. Afterward, new glazes and body styles were developed. Marblehead Pottery's designs and quality craftsmanship was quickly recognized and the company received many awards over the years. (Levin 1988, 118-120)

In 1925, Arthur Baggs would begin to divide his time between Marblehead and Cowan Pottery. Marblehead Pottery would cease production in 1936. (Levin 1988, 140)

Marks, Saturday Evening Girls and Paul Revere. *Courtesy of Naomi's of San Francisco.*

Saturday Evening Girls/Paul Revere wares. Back: Cup, Blue, 1923, 5.25" high. $185. Plate, lighter Blue, 8.5" diameter. $135. Plate, Blue, 1921, 7 1/2" diameter. $125. Front: Cream and sugar service (features both marks), Yellow, 1923. Pitcher, 3.25" high, sugar bowl, 3" high at lid knob, $385/set. Paul Revere (new name for SEG) candlesticks, Blue Green, 6.25" high, $545/pair. Saturday Evening Girls items are dated. After the name change to Paul Revere, the dating of the wares largely comes to a halt. While a number of these items may be a little early for this period, they have the same spirit and are simply too interesting to pass by. *Courtesy of Naomi's of San Francisco.*

Mark, Marblehead. *Courtesy of Naomi's of San Francisco.*

Saturday Evening Girls/Paul Revere wares. Vase, aqua, c. 1919, 7.25" high. $425. Shallow bowl, pink, c. 1919, 6.75". $225. Flower frog, Yellow, approx. 3" diameter. $85. Vase, Green, c. 1920, 6.75" high. $375. *Courtesy of Naomi's of San Francisco.*

Marblehead ceramics. Left to right: vase, pink, 3.5" high, $300+; bowl, Yellow, 3.75" high x 5.75" diameter, $600; bowl, Blue, 2.25" high x 6.5" diameter, $350+; vase, Yellow, 5.5" high, $350+; small vase, purple, 4.25" high, $350+; and vase, Blue, 4.5" high x 5.5" diameter, $300+. *Courtesy of Naomi's of San Francisco.*

CAMARK ART AND TILE POTTERY

In 1926, Camark was founded by Samuel Carnes in Camden, Arkansas. The firm's art director, John Lessell, produced striking lustre and iridescent wares. With the advent of the Depression, the business was sold, but production continued. In the 1930s, Camark turned to the manufacture of utilitarian wares, simple commercial cast items, and a number of popular novelty wares. Also produced were a variety of decorated artwares, bowls, planters, and vases.

The pottery was again sold in 1962, struggling on with diminishing sales until 1982, when the Camark potting firm was closed. (Cox 1996, 42)

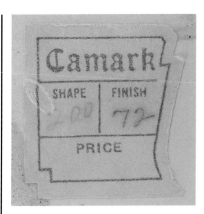

Camark paper label mark. *Courtesy of Naomi's of San Francisco.*

Fish bowl novelty item by Camark, 8.5" high. $185. *Courtesy of Naomi's of San Francisco.*

This is an interesting story. The University of North Dakota began the School of Mines in 1890. Native North Dakota clay was required for use in the pottery; however, eastern companies were found to produce the wares from clays sent them by Earle Babcock (director since 1898). Among the eastern potteries involved were the Zanesville, Ohio, firms of Roseville Pottery Company, Ohio Pottery Company, and J.B. Owens Pottery Company. Upon return of the wares, native North Dakota artists would decorate the items from time to time.

In 1910, Margaret Kelly Cable came on board as the principal instructor for a new ceramics department. Known for the wares she produced with a distinctive Art Deco styling, Cable retired in 1949.

Wares produced by in this endeavor are most commonly marked with a cobalt seal reading "University of North Dakota Grand Forks, N.D. Made at School of Mines N.D. Clay." Artists frequently signed their items, either with their name or initials. Students who studied pottery manufacture at the University marked their names or initials on pottery as well. (Cox 1996, 158)

University of North Dakota School of Mines mark. *Courtesy of Naomi's of San Francisco.*

North Dakota School of Mines ceramics. Teapot, Brown, 5" high at knob. Cream and sugar service, Brown, sugar bowl 3.25" at knob, pitcher, 2.25" at rim. $725/set. Pair of planter bookends, Yellow Ochre with Brown leaf design, 3.75" high. $485/pair. Small vase, Red, 4" high. $240. *Courtesy of Naomi's of San Francisco.*

PISGAH FOREST POTTERY

Walter Stephen established his Pisgah Forest Pottery in Arden, North Carolina, in 1926. Here Stephen created a range of high fired vitrified hand made pottery wares in a variety of glaze colors, including a crystalline glaze. Frequently, the crystalline glazes were applied with two or three colors on an object. Pisgah Forest wares were also decorated with scenes of American pioneers involved in a variety of activities from square dancing to buffalo hunting.

Pisgah Forest Pottery produced candle sticks, cups and saucers, cream and sugar sets, mugs, pitchers, teapots and vases. Miniature pieces may also be found. This pottery's wares are consistently marked and dated.

After Walter Stephen's death in 1961, the pottery was continued on a part time basis by Tom Case and Grady Ledbetter. (Henzke 1996, 182-183)

Mark, Pisgah Forest. *Courtesy of Naomi's of San Francisco.*

Pisgah Forest ceramics. Bowl, Turquoise, 3" high. $115. Vase, Turquoise, 5" high. $95. Cream and sugar service, Green, creamer, 3.5" high, sugar bowl with lid, 4.5" high at lid knob. $125/set. Vase, Light Blue, 4.75" high. $95. Vase, Light Blue, 3.75" high. $145. *Courtesy of Naomi's of San Francisco.*

PINE RIDGE

Margaret Kelly Cable, the principal instructor in the University of North Dakota ceramics department, taught pottery techniques to the Sioux Indians from 1931 until 1949. Together Cable and her Sioux students produced simple, utilitarian ware—not always decorated with Indian motifs.

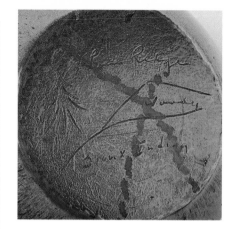

Mark, Pine Ridge. *Courtesy of Naomi's of San Francisco.*

Pine Ridge pitcher, bowl, and vase. Pitcher, 4.25" high. $75. Bowl, 2" high x 6.75" diameter. $165. Vase, 4.5" high. $165. *Courtesy of Naomi's of San Francisco.*

Pine Ridge bud vase and mug. Bud vase, Brown and cream, 8.5" high. $265. Mug, rust and cream, 3.75" high. $165. *Courtesy of Naomi's of San Francisco.*

BIBLIOGRAPHY

Bassett, Mark. *Introducing Roseville Pottery*. Atglen, Pennsylvania: Schiffer Publishing, 1999.

Bauer, Cheryl. "Bauer staked claim early in Calif. pottery run." *Antique Week*, April 8, 1996, pp. 1 & 48.

Burns, Jr., Thomas A. "Hall China still a practical addition to kitchen." *Antique Week*, March 25, 1996, pp. 1, 41, & 43.

Chipman, Jack. *Collector's Encyclopedia of California Pottery. Second Edition*. Paducah, Kentucky: Collector Books, 1999.

Coleman, Karin. "Roseville Pottery. A Beginner's Point of View" *Antiques & Collecting Magazine*, March 1994, No. 99 (1), pp. 34-37.

Ellis, Anita J. *Rookwood Pottery. The Glaze Lines*. Atglen, Pennsylvania: Schiffer Publishing, 1995.

Gilchrist, Brenda (ed.). *The Smithsonian Illustrated Library of Antiques. Pottery*. Washington, D.C.: Smithsonian Institution, 1981.

Hay, Jane. *Christie's Collectibles. Art Deco Ceramics. The Connoisseur's Guide*. Boston, Massachusetts: Little, Brown and Company, 1996.

Henzke, Lucile. *Art Pottery of America*. Atglen, Pennsylvania: Schiffer Publishing, 1996. [Original printing 1982]

Huxford, Sharon and Bob. *The Collector's Encyclopedia of Roseville Pottery*. Paducah, Kentucky: Collector Books, 1995 (update of 1976 original).

Johnson, Bruce E. "Bauer Pottery." *Country Living*, April 1996, No. 19 (4), pp. 48-51.

Levin, Elaine. *The History of American Ceramics, 1607 to the Present. From Pipkins and Bean Pots to Contemporary Forms*. New York: Harry N. Abrams, Inc., 1988.

McDonald, Ann Gilbert. "The Working Women of Weller. The Story of Two Weller Artists During the Great Depression." *Antiques & Collecting Magazine*, October 1997 No. 102 (8), p. 18-21.

Piña, Leslie. *Pottery. Modern Wares. 1920-1960*. Atglen, Pennsylvania: Schiffer Publishing, 1994.

Richey, Tina A. "Fulper Pottery." *Antiques & Collecting Magazine*. January 1999, pp. 38-45.

Snyder, Jeffrey B. *Fiesta: Homer Laughlin China Company's Colorful Dinnerware*. Atglen, Pennsylvania: Schiffer Publishing, 1999 2nd Revised and Expanded Edition.

_____. *Franciscan Dining Services*. Atglen, Pennsylvania: Schiffer Publishing, 1996.

Whitmyer, Margaret & Kenn. *The Collector's Encyclopedia of Hall China*. Paducah, Kentucky: Collector Books, 1989.

INDEX